GW01316312

Praise
Our Father Who

'Carlin's memoir and detective
and a deeply resonant eloquence, a precious and very rare
combination. Reading it is both a punch in the gut and a
tender caress. It is a pleasure to take my hat off to him.'

CHRISTOS TSIOLKAS

'In an act of great empathy and imagination, David Carlin both creates
a father, and fully illuminates the experience of fatherlessness.'

JOAN LONDON

'David Carlin ... draws on official records and family memories
to create a moving portrait of a troubled man, filling in the gaps
with a yearning imagination. It is a beautifully realised book.'

AUSTRALIAN LITERARY REVIEW BLOG

'An ingenious and insightful memoir ... It's a brilliant set-up, because
Carlin's moving story centres on the search for another who had to
exist, logically, but of whom he had no memory: his father, Brian.'

STEPHEN ROMEI, *THE WEEKEND AUSTRALIAN*

'Factual research is blended seamlessly with the vivid
imaginings of a lyrical and compassionate storyteller ... This
courageous and insightful book will resonate strongly.'

SIAN PRIOR, *THE AGE*

'In part evocative family memoir, part detective story ... Carlin
produces a fine study of a family and its secrets.'

LUCY SUSSEX, *SUNDAY AGE*

'*Our Father Who Wasn't There* is less about the real man and more about
Carlin's deep longing for him. Such a search is a shell game, ever elusive,
impossible to win, but a loving and beautifully written tribute nonetheless.'

ADAIR JONES, *COURIER MAIL*

More praise for

Our Father Who Wasn't There

'This is an affecting and beautifully written memoir.'
SUNDAY TELEGRAPH

'Compelling reading.'
SUNDAY MAGAZINE (SUNDAY HERALD SUN)

'The delight of this book is in how Carlin adjusts the perspective
to help or hinder the interpretation of truth ... I consider a
memoir a cumulative narrative that ultimately proffers some
revelation or illumination and this one does so with such a
delightful concluding whimper it could almost be a bang.'
JEREMY FISHER, SYDNEY MORNING HERALD

'*Our Father Who Wasn't There* is a compelling, beautifully written, and
deeply felt homage to the ghost of a father for whom a son still mourns.'
ROD MORAN, WEST AUSTRALIAN

David Carlin is a Melbourne-based writer, creative artist, teacher and researcher. He is author of the memoir *Our Father Who Wasn't There* (2010) and his creative nonfiction, essays and articles have appeared in *Griffith Review, Overland, Text, Newswrite, Victorian Writer, Continuum* and other journals. David is co-director of the nonfictionLab at RMIT University. He has previously written and directed for theatre, film and circus, and since 2008 has led the *Circus Oz Living Archive* project.

David Carlin

The Abyssinian Contortionist

Hope, friendship and other circus acts

For Vesna

Lovely to meet you +
looking forward to
more non/fiction
conversations.

U W
A P
UWA PUBLISHING

First published in 2015 by
UWA Publishing
Crawley, Western Australia 6009
www.uwap.uwa.edu.au

THE UNIVERSITY OF
WESTERN AUSTRALIA

A full CIP data entry is available from the National Library of Australia

ISBN: 978-1-74258-678-6

Photograph of Sosina Wogayehu © Angela McConnell
Typeset in Bembo by Lasertype
Printed by Griffin

For Linda and Melaku,
Esther, Louis, Raeey and Kidus

CONTENTS

Prologue

The cigarette seller of Addis Ababa works her corner near the entrance to the brewery. She buys her cigarettes by the packet at the wholesale shop a twenty-minute walk away, and sells them one by one to the men who pass by on the street. Some days a man will buy a whole packet at once and she has made an afternoon's fortune in a minute.

In the beginning, the cigarette seller of Addis Ababa needs only enough capital to buy her first packet, and somehow she has enough. She works her corner in the afternoons after school.

The cigarette seller lives with her family in the compound of the St George beer factory because her father has an important job there. He is responsible for the smooth running of all of the beer-making machinery. If anything goes wrong, day or night, the cigarette seller's father has to fix it.

Her father's job is so important that, if he goes to the stadium to watch the St George soccer team on a Saturday afternoon, which he loves to do, he has to tell his men in which section and in which row of the stadium he will be sitting, so that, if there is a problem with the machinery, one of them can run into the stadium during the soccer match and fetch him from his seat. They don't have mobile phones at this time, in Addis Ababa or anywhere.

Her father's job is so important that, two times, His Royal Highness the Emperor Haile Selasse (to use only the bare minimum of his titles) came to the St George brewery in his imperial vehicle, a luxury car imported from Europe, and paid her father his monthly salary in person. The Emperor Haile Selasse happens to be the owner of the St George brewery. He is remarkably small and slight, as everybody knows, but he has a power. The entire world respects him. He stood up to Mussolini. It is said that he is descended in a direct line from King Solomon and the Queen of Sheba. Even if this hasn't been confirmed, it is true he has a power.

The cigarette seller doesn't tell her father she is selling cigarettes. He wouldn't want his daughter selling cigarettes. No other girls sell cigarettes.

She doesn't care what other girls do. She has no interest in the dolls they play with. She will never be able to make coffee properly. Even when she is eighteen years old, if her mother asks her to make coffee, she will straddle the coffee pot with her legs apart on the ground, and her mother will tell her to get out. Her mother will never enjoy watching her make coffee in this fashion.

Being on the street enables the cigarette seller to understand people when they are drunk. This knowledge will come in handy sometimes, later in her life.

If she has sold enough cigarettes for the afternoon, the cigarette seller plays table soccer or ping-pong with the boys, her friends in the street who make money washing cars, barefoot in the dust. All the bad boys are her friends because she can do tricks. She can show them things she has learnt from Bruce Lee movies. She can do the splits and she can hit them. Also, she can read their minds. They are not so scary. They are too afraid to hit her like they hit her sister.

The cigarette seller's sister will always be in trouble. She is too beautiful. She is six years older but, when the cigarette seller is eight, the older sister asks the younger to teach her how to do a walkover. A walkover is like a cartwheel with one hand. The cigarette seller spends time trying to teach her sister how to do a walkover. Her sister is hopeless. She is the opposite of the cigarette seller. She is clean, decent and prays all the time, every night and every morning. She says, 'Thank God for the day we have had.' The cigarette seller doesn't thank God every night for her earnings.

She says to her sister: 'I've taught you everything about how to do a walkover and now it's up to you.' But her sister is hopeless. The boys hit her. She is too beautiful.

After this, the sister stays always near the lounge room of their home. She makes it spotless.

The sister has beautiful clothes, which the cigarette seller loves to wear sometimes. They are actually exactly the same as her own clothes, but bigger. She prefers them. Because they are much too big for her, she ties them up with a belt. She steals her sister's clothes, ties them up with a belt, and jumps out of her sister's window. Her mother catches her and threatens: 'Don't you ever do that again!'

But, even though the cigarette seller says she never will, the next day she is out of the window again with her sister's clothes on and the belt. The cigarette seller is scared of nothing.

She has left her house since she was eight years old to sell her cigarettes. She is not like any other girls. At the St George Elementary School, which lies on the same road as the beer factory but on the other side, she sits at the front in class and cleans the blackboard. She is covered in white dust but doesn't care.

If her older sister stays out until after seven in the evening, her parents are worried about where she is. The cigarette seller tells her parents: 'You don't like me. That's why you don't worry where *I* am.'

Her mother tells her: 'You are not the daughter of me! You are the daughter of Chagago!' The cigarette seller knows very well that Chagago is the mad guy down the street. When Chagago comes by, all the kids run.

The cigarette seller of Addis Ababa does well at her trade. She looks like a boy, with her hair cropped short, but people are more likely to buy from her than from the boys. She is loud. She sings, she dances and does flips. It is very hard for the others to compete with this cigarette seller. She is business-oriented.

The cigarette seller diversifies. She sells small pastries in plastic wrappers and chewing gum as well as cigarettes.

She shares her money with her friends. She takes them out to buy *espris* – rainbow-striped juices, thick as soup, with layers of papaya, guava, mango, banana and avocado.

She shares her money with the boys who wash the cars and the others who sell things with her outside the compound. If they have no money of their own she buys goods from the wholesaler for them to sell.

At home the cigarette seller is never still, even if she is watching Bruce Lee and German variety shows on television. She is always wrestling with her brothers or using the beds as trampolines.

Her brothers who, afterwards, will be lost or far away.

She has a problem to be still. She is of no use to her mother. Before Easter, there is two months' fasting. All this time, the cigarette seller's family eats no meat or dairy. At the end there is a feast, where the family, which is large, eats four chickens. There is a certain way to cut each chicken into twelve pieces before cooking, a very certain way it must be done. The cigarette seller's mother gives a chicken to each child so that each of them can learn how to split the chicken properly. But the cigarette seller never learns how to split a chicken properly. She says to her mother: 'I need to go to the toilet.' Then she climbs out of the window and doesn't come back.

The St George soccer team lives in a house in the cigarette seller's compound at the brewery. One of the families moved out and the St George football team moved in. Whenever the St George football team goes for training, the cigarette seller hops on to their bus. She trains with them. They kick the ball and she does flips and bends her body into shapes. They say to her, 'Come on, Mimi,' – because *mimi*, little girl, is her nickname – 'Come on, Mimi, show us some tricks. Show us a dog, a cat, a six. A nine.' The cigarette seller knows all of these tricks and more.

Inside the entrance to the compound of the St George brewery is a pub. You can buy dinner there, and St George beer from the tap. It is the freshest beer in Addis.

One day, the managers of the St George brewery pub go to visit the cigarette seller's father, at his office. They are angry. They have collected up all the empty plastic wrappers from the pastries that the cigarette seller has sold. They show the plastic wrappers to the cigarette seller's father: 'Your daughter is taking over our business! We are losing customers – look at how many pastries she is selling. This many in a day!'

They wave all the plastic wrappers at him.

But the cigarette seller's father says to them: 'Calm down. My daughter wouldn't do that.'

He goes home and says to the cigarette seller: 'Sit here and tell me honestly what you are up to. Are you selling cigarettes, and these pastries with the wrappers?'

'Yes.' She says straight out. 'Yes, I sell the cigarettes. I sell everything.'

The cigarette seller's father asks her to stop selling.

'I don't want to stop,' she says.

Then they have a very big argument. She tells him that she is not going to stop because there are a lot of poor kids who live outside the compound and she shares her money with them. If she sells something, she shares her money with the other kids who are trying to make money by cleaning cars. 'So,' she says, 'it is not only for me, because I share it with the other kids, and I am not going to stop this.'

The cigarette seller's father tries to negotiate a peace between the managers of the St George pub and the cigarette seller. He brings them together to discuss the situation. He says to the managers of the pub: 'Don't worry, she is not going to sell the things inside the compound; she is only going to sell them outside the front gate, so it should be fine.'

The managers are still not happy.

The cigarette seller's father becomes angry with the managers now. He says to them: 'Do you think, if somebody is coming here to eat a roast at your pub, they are just going to eat that little pastry instead and leave? Are you that stupid?'

And he walks off.

The managers all call out after him: 'We don't want to see her around here any more! Okay?'

The cigarette seller's father comes right back to them and says: 'This is her compound; this is where she lives and where she plays and you can't stop her being here.'

And the cigarette seller says to the managers – who have all shaken hands with the Emperor Haile Selasse, the owner of the St George pub and brewery who in turn may be directly descended from King Solomon and the Queen of Sheba and certainly, at this time at least, has a power that emanates from every fibre of his diminutive body – she says to these imperial hotel managers: 'I am going to sell my cigarettes right here from my own front door, behind the gate of our house, here inside the compound, and nobody can stop me because I am still inside my house.'

The managers don't know how to deal with this cigarette seller, who is so small and insignificant but seems also to have a power.

The cigarette seller's father asks her one more time. 'Just stop this thing and go to school and when you finish school I will try to put you in a good job,' he says. But the cigarette seller is very strict with her father: she tells him that if wants to put anybody in a good job it should be her sister, who is beautiful but has already left school and doesn't have a job. 'Don't worry about me,' says the cigarette seller, 'I can get myself a job. I can do any job. You don't need to put me in a job.'

Her father sighs and says to her: 'You are not like any ordinary kid.' He wonders where she came from, how she came to be his daughter.

But actually this brings about a remarkable change in the cigarette seller's father, hitherto very strict and unbending in his family, and never known to change his mind. Now someone else in the family is unbending in her beliefs, but on top of that a very good negotiator. The cigarette seller's father learns from his own daughter how to negotiate and be flexible.

Her mother says to her: 'You're making money, but now you need to start saving money.'

Her mother says to her: 'You need to start an *ekube*.'

An *ekube* is a traditional system for saving money in Ethiopia. The cigarette seller knows already how one works. You gather together a group of people and each agrees to put in so much money once a month. Every month it will be the turn of a different member of the group to draw out all the money put in that month, and use it as needed. You all come together and socialise, drink coffee, bring along your monthly savings and place them in the pot. The one whose turn it is to draw out the money each month has been determined at the beginning of the *ekube* by the picking of the names out one by one: first name, first month, and so on. And if the January person doesn't want to take their money in January they can sell it to the October person, minus ten per cent.

But the cigarette seller's mother organises it so that the cigarette seller's name comes out last in her *ekube*. She will receive her money only in the final month.

There are twelve people in this *ekube*, including the cigarette seller. Every month the twelve will each put in 100 birr.

In Ethiopia there are thirteen months every year, and every year starts seven years, eight months and eleven days later than the same year in the Gregorian calendar, but for leap years when they wait one day more. The cigarette seller of Addis Ababa lives always in the past.

The months have thirty days, save for the last, Pagumen, which has only five. Naturally this short, stubby month does not count in the *ekube*.

After a year has gone by, the cigarette seller's mother hands her, one day, an envelope with 1200 birr inside. The cigarette seller is speechless. She doesn't know what to do with all this money.

She says: 'I'm going to give it to my dad.'

Growing up in Ethiopia, it is every child's wish to give money to their family. There is no welfare system.

The father of the cigarette seller is sitting in the lounge room watching television when she brings him in her gift. He looks inside the envelope and at his little girl, this cigarette seller with her cropped hair and her spunk. Then he cries and cries for ages, because he has been against her selling cigarettes the whole time.

He wonders again where this cigarette seller came from; how she came to be his daughter. He asks the grandmother of the cigarette seller to come to bless her; to bless his child for God to give her everything she wants. The grandmother is the elder of the family and age has made her wise; therefore, she is best equipped for blessings.

The cigarette seller's name is Sosina. (She has other names, too; but, as we will see later, precisely what they are is liable to change.)

1

Hurdy-gurdy

So this is sort of how it happened.

Sosina said to me: 'How about it, Dave?'

I was walking to the flat Sosina shared with her husband, Mel, in the Housing Commission high-rises of Carlton, inner-north Melbourne, Australia.

I had never been inside these Housing Commission flats before, and was a little nervous at the prospect – on guard for drug-dealers and muggers. These flats, like their post-war cousins elsewhere, the abandoned children of Le Corbusier, are decrepit now, windswept castles with invisible battlements to keep the poor, the mad and the newly migrated isolated from the chic bars and cafés springing up all round.

I ride my bicycle to work at the university each weekday through the grounds of the Housing Commission flats. In the morning I see the Somali mothers in their hijabs, walking their kids to the little public school on the edge of the flats, the school that the middle-class families avoid.

Opposite the school, at the southern end of the flats, is a church that doles out soup sometimes. The mosque is a much longer walk away, in the other direction, along Drummond Street. Built by the expatriate Albanian community, its slender minaret towers incongruously above the Victorian terrace houses of Carlton North.

Sosi had given me instructions: which building to enter, which lift to take, which floor to get out on. The foyer for the lifts was cold and grimy brown. A middle-aged man occupied a bench opposite the twin lift doors, hunched and distant. I thought to myself, idly, *If the lift doors open and a young man steps in, do I follow? What are the chances he will knife me in the lift against the mirror?* I occasionally have such idle knifing thoughts; I imagine how surprised my face would look as the blade slid into me.

I rode up to the eleventh floor alone and came out onto an open landing. Like a hotel turned inside out, the building's corridors run on its exterior. Heavy mesh had been erected above the concrete railings, as if to say the urge to fly downwards or to push one's *fucking wife* or *fucking neighbour* over to a bloody death had often enough been too hard to resist.

Nothing stirred on the eleventh floor.

I knocked on the door that bore the number Sosi had given me. Immediately, it swung open and she embraced me with her familiar gusto. 'Hi, Dave! Come in!'

The flat, a small oasis, shimmered in the late afternoon light from the west-facing windows. A large red-leather couch set and a flat screen TV crowded the living room.

'Look at our beautiful view!' said Sosi. Through the golden haze I could make out the Westgate Bridge and the distant hills of the You Yangs.

Sosi made me Ethiopian coffee, strong, black and sweet. I sat at the dining room table and looked at the large framed wedding photos on the wall. Sosi and Mel posed resplendent in their formal outfits, like royalty.

Mel, she told me, was sleeping in the bedroom. He worked the night shift at a biscuit factory in Kensington, as well as studying for his degree in computer networking and helping out with the Footscray community at the African Youth Centre.

Sosi poured the boiling water onto the coffee in the traditional ceramic pot, dun-coloured with a narrow open neck that also served as a handle, and a separate spout. She tilted the pot on its side towards the spout, and left it to brew, balanced on a stand. When she poured the coffee she took care to keep the pot tilted, so that the sediment remained undisturbed at the bottom.

'Why do you want to tell your story in a book?' I asked. 'Why precisely?'

'Because people don't see me for who I am. If I say I am Ethiopian, people only think of 1984: the famine, starving children. They are so surprised to look at me: you are a *well-fed* Ethiopian girl! They ask: do you have a house? Do you have pet elephants? Pet tigers?'

She looked at me, incredulous.

'We get asked about kangaroos,' I nodded.

She smiled and pointed at the bowl of vegetable stew.

'Do you like the sauce? We call that *wat*. Is it too hot for you? Coffee?'

She poured more coffee into my cup and munched on a scrap of *injera*, the ubiquitous Ethiopian bread.

She told me that she had a name in mind for the book: 'Short Black'. This refers both to her height and skin, and to the cultural significance of coffee in her birth land of Ethiopia – for Ethiopia is coffee's birth land, too. Not South America, as I had vaguely thought.

'I have a subtitle for the book, too,' she said: 'Tales of an Abyssinian girl. It's better to say Abyssinian instead of Ethiopian,

because they will not think only of 1984. How about it, Dave?'
she said, and looked at me with her clear brown eyes.

Usually I hate being called Dave…

Sosina and I first met among trapeze bars and tightwire walkers.
We were both working for Circus Oz, a contemporary circus – the
sort without animals or sawdust – and something of an institution
in Australia. You can search it up, as my son, Louis, would say.

Sosina, having long since ceased to surprise her parents back
in Ethiopia, had walked into the job as a performer, straight out
of the new Australian national circus school. I was helping to
direct their new show. I'd directed Circus Oz once before but,
unlike Sosina, wasn't really a circus type. My background and
training had been in theatre and, personally, I had a positive terror
of attempting anything more acrobatic than a forward roll.

Sosina came into Circus Oz as a contortionist and juggler,
and her act was one of those I was responsible for directing. In
practice, this meant I mainly stayed out of the way and made
encouraging noises as she and aerialist Anni Davey devised a new
hybrid contortion and trapeze act.

The lights come up on Sosina rotating on a small disc lit with
footlights. She is dressed as if in a nineteenth-century travelling
show; the circus musicians stand close by, playing hurdy-gurdy
music as she twists her body inside and out. The Big Top is
crowded, hushed. Sosina comes to a rest in some enfolded pose,
from which Anni, who has been lowered towards the stage
upside down on a trapeze bar, grasps and lifts her into the air as
the ropes of the trapeze are hoisted up again. In the air above
the ring, the two of them twist in each other's arms with Anni
(strong as two women) bearing the weight of Sosina, until the
latter settles her body into a new impossible position and is once
more deposited on the disc, there to slowly spin, hurdy-gurdy,

hurdy-gurdy, shoulders onto ankles, eyes staring out between her thighs.

Sosina's gaze, calm and even, catches the audience just as they catch her; this is the act, really. Contortion makes the body strange and freakish, and this is an African body, too, in front of a largely white audience, so it is stranger still, tickling distant memories buried deep within the culture. Isn't she a little like a (whisper it) *golliwog*, with her raggle-taggle hair and floppy limbs? The dolls our mothers played with; the dolls I, David, remember from my Australian childhood in the sixties. Everything had its place in the corner pile of porcelain and cloth and wool. Even little Golly! She could join in, too, although she was altogether different and came from somewhere far away in the jungles and the deserts where Mowgli lived and Little Black Sambo, too, the *dark* boy who ran and ran in circles and melted into butter with the tiger chasing him. Or did the yellow tiger melt? They all melted together in the jungles of a child's mind and the glimmer of a starchy hardback (hurdy-gurdy).

Sosina on her spinning disc among the light bulbs is, in the depths of some white eyes, the golliwog brought to life. But she looks right back at us, her audience, and says: Well, actually, you have *no idea who I am*; but that's okay, because it's *my* show now that you are watching.

At first glance, there is nothing about Sosina and me that is the same. She is short, I am tall; she is black, I am white; she's a woman, I'm a man. She was born in just about the poorest country in the world, I in affluent Australia. She can bounce-juggle eight balls on a block of marble; I – well, I can juggle three balls. In my hands.

That's my greatest circus trick and I'm quite proud of it. It has variations: the basic pattern, the outside-in, the upside down, the snazzy one – where you throw one of the balls especially high in the air and pause or do a twirl – and the joke pattern, in which one hand juggles two balls while the other moves the third ball up and down alongside, doing no juggling at all. If you do the joke pattern well, the audience falls for the illusion, even if only for a moment, before they see the trick, and before they realise that you are happy for them to see the trick.

But I cannot begin to imagine being able to juggle eight balls, what it must take to master such a skill. Not only the hours of single-minded practice, but the obsession, the yogic focus. Sosina says she loves to train her hands to do things really fast. When she had a job for a few weeks selling popcorn front of house, one of her tasks was to fold the paper cups for the popcorn into shape. She became obsessed with the choreography of the task. She analysed the exact sequence of movements required to fold one paper cup. Once she had it down, she worked on going faster. And faster. She would come in early to work and fold a whole stack of cups, far more than she needed to, quicker than anyone else would dream of. She turned the act of folding paper cups into a feat. A meditation. A private art form.

Sosina's told me that, ever since she first came across contortionists, magicians, jugglers, knife-throwers and all the rest, at the age of six, sitting on the floor of her parents' lounge room in Addis Ababa, gazing at the once-a-week German variety show on the only television channel in the land, she knew that she wanted to master such tricks for herself, no matter how long it took, and to perform them wherever and whenever she could find an audience, in all the great and far-off corners of the world. And she has done it.

Maybe it was exactly because of this chasm of difference between us that I felt myself drawn more and more to the idea of making a book with Sosina; a book that tried to trace the contours of that gap. This, I thought, would be my 'not me' book. I had already written a book about me – about my family, my father, his suicide and how I missed it, being only six months old when it occurred, and about nobody afterwards ever mentioning it, or him, and how I had this overwhelming drive to make them all tell me everything they knew about his life and death, no matter how bad it was, and this overwhelming drive, too, to write the story down, have others read it – and, yes, I suppose that includes others in all the great and far-off corners of the world.

This book would be about Sosina, the epitome of 'not me'. But it would also feel wrong to pretend I wasn't involved, to pretend that telling, making and sharing stories across cultures isn't complicated. In Circus Oz they never hide the rigging in their acts.

I wondered what kind of book we could make together. What would be its bones and its intestines. Sosi, early on, lent me a couple of recent autobiographies of African women, stories of extraordinary courage and hardship: female circumcision, war, bloodshed. Triumph over circumstance. Stories that went inexorably, for better or worse, from A to B. I couldn't get into them. I felt I knew already what they were telling me, just not the details. We turn on the TV; we see current affairs reports of far-off pain and suffering. On the other channel is the tennis. I almost certainly didn't give those books the attention that those women's stories merit. But half the world's problems, maybe more than that, are about getting somebody to pay attention, aren't they?

The bookselling industry has a category I've come across in airport bookshops called *Misery Biography*. The counterpoint on the adjacent shelf is *Entertainment Biography*. But are those really the only two types of life-stories we are interested in?

'I don't think I want to do it quite like that,' I said to Sosi. 'You know, straight, like that.'

'Sure,' she said. 'I don't mind. We can do it how we like.'

Sosina is an artist. In a circus, it's all about trust. If your partner drops you, you might be dead.

Thus together, but from completely different places, we set out.

2

True love at gunpoint

To see Sosina's mother and father, Ayanalem and Tewabé, married so long and happily, you wouldn't think it all started with a kidnapping. True love at gunpoint – and Ayanalem, her mother, aged only fourteen, back in the 1960s when Haile Selassie was his most Imperial Highness in Ethiopia and seemed like he always would be.

Tewabé grew up in the countryside, in a simple one-room hut on a farm outside a small village in the province of Shewa, 160 kilometres from Addis Ababa. When he was a boy he knew only of the farm and his family, the animals – goats, sheep, chickens – and the bush all around. The sound of hyenas in the moonlight.

He was born into Ethiopia's Italian occupation in the 1930s, which in the end came and went quickly because Mussolini did so badly in World War II. Tewabé was raised on the stories his mother told him of those days. The men of the area they lived in were fierce warriors, she told him, which prevented the Italian troops from coming through and burning all the houses down. Instead the Italians set up a camp outside the village, to which the women of the village brought fresh eggs and milk and other food they'd grown, to fill the soldier's bellies and keep war out of their minds. Tewabé's mother carried eggs to the Italians while her stomach was swollen with him inside. The Italian soldiers were so touched that they gave her in return 100 kilograms of sugar and many bags of coffee to take home. Tewabé became known as the lucky boy, the rich boy, as if it was he who had brought these unheard-of riches to his family when really it was his mother all along.

Tewabé's mother told him later: 'Your grandfather once played a trick on the Italians. One day they captured him in the street on his way to church and forced him, with a dozen others, to lead them across the rocky countryside to Minjat, a place they wanted to invade. The Italians forced your grandfather and the others to walk all day until nightfall.' In the evening, she told him, they stopped to sleep in a field, and the Italians gave their Ethiopian prisoner guides a cow to share between them for their dinner. The Ethiopians, choosing their best moment, stabbed the cow with a small knife, just enough to make her angry and run away. Pretending to chase after her, they fled in the black night all the way home to their villages, leaving the Italians lost in the bush and dreaming, no doubt, of hyenas. Not to mention lions.

His mother sent Tewabé to the church school in the local town, the only sort of school available. He learnt the two hundred different letters of Amharic and how to read and write with them. From the alphabet and calendar, he graduated to prayers and Bible stories. The children lived in the rooms of the school that clustered around the church and relied on their relatives, such as Tewabé's elder sister, to send them food.

As Tewabé grew older he was given more duties in the service of the church. He helped to organise the christenings and weddings, the weekly prayers. This was the unpaid work expected of every boy who wanted an education but couldn't pay for it. Tewabé would have continued happily to serve the church, eventually travelling the 500 kilometres to the town where the higher learning of the church was conducted, attaining the best education possible and one day becoming a priest; but when he was fourteen his elder sister died, and with her his means of support. He could no longer afford his life of study. Tewabé pulled up all the vegetables he had been growing on a plot of land for his sister, sold them at the market, and ran away to Addis Ababa with the money.

It was enough to get him to his aunt's.

As Tewabé is telling us this story, Sosina and I are sitting at the dining table in his unadorned linoleum-floored lounge room, which from my point of view is simply somewhere in the vast reaches of Addis Ababa where if not for Sosina I would be as lost as those Italians. Tewabé speaks Amharic; Sosina translates for me.

The night I first met Tewabé, a few days earlier, he was spread out on the couch in the same room, watching Manchester United on cable TV. The television was positioned on a cabinet above one end of the couch so that he could lie down and gaze at it above his feet. He got up and shook my hand, professing not to speak English. Sosina translated our simple greetings, and he turned back to the football.

Tewabé seemed at first somewhat marginal in the family, just another of the many household satellites orbiting his wife, Ayanalem. He didn't appear to do much. Only later would I come to appreciate his quiet energy. He was lean and fit, looking younger than his sixty-eight years. Sosina told me he had built each and every building in the small compound – the house, hotel, café and restaurant – with his own hands and those of his son Amaha (Sosina's brother). The masonry, the plastering, the plumbing, the wiring, everything. DIY is not a weekend hobby in Ethiopia; it's the only way a middle-class family like Sosina's can afford to get things done.

At the age of nineteen, staying with his aunt in Addis Ababa, Tewabé enrolled in elementary school (clearly his previous schooling had had its limitations). He didn't care that the other students were all aged around six. He studied for three years in elementary school, skipping a grade every year to reach Grade Six in record time. But he began to have disagreements, of one sort or another, living with his aunt. He might have been in elementary school but he was a young man, not a child. He moved out of her house to look for work.

At this point, a miraculous *deus ex machina*, in the shape of the world-famous Ethiopian marathon runner Abebe Bikila, landed in the story. It was 1953 in the Ethiopian calendar and Abebe Bikila was returning in triumph to his homeland, having won the marathon in the Rome Olympics, barefoot. Tewabé and his friends walked all morning through the rambling backblocks of the city and out into the country fields to reach the tiny airport. They watched the plane descending from the clouds, held their breath as its wheels bumped against the ground, and cheered as the world champion stepped out onto the tarmac. As they tromped back to the city afterwards they happened to pass the St George brewery and noticed a mass of men outside. The brewery had put out a call that very day, seeking new workers.

Tewabé added his name to the list outside the brewery. A few days later he was given a job (behind the scenes, his aunt had begged on his behalf to someone she knew who worked there). He began by carrying boxes of beer to the brewery warehouse, on a wage of 75 Ethiopian cents (0.75 birr) a day. He had never been happier, he says, for life was cheap back then. He and his friends each paid a man 12 birr to feed them for a whole month, and still had money left to buy beer and cigarettes.

Tewabé rose up quickly through the ranks as his intelligence and talents became apparent. First they made him an apprentice to the chief technician of the factory, then an assistant technician. He had a gift for anything mechanical.

He got to know a man named Mola. Together with his brother and other members of their family, Mola occupied the higher echelons of management. Mola was a boss Tewabé held in high esteem, a man of principle, dignity and refinement. This was a man with whom it would be an honour to be related. And wasn't that Mola's daughter, the graceful young girl he saw coming and going from the brewery? Could Tewabé permit himself to dream? Over weeks and months the idea of marriage, at first fanciful, grew stronger in his head.

Tewabé didn't overestimate his chances as a suitor. Coming from a poor family in the countryside, he had no good family connections in Addis. Who did he think he was: an ordinary workingman asking to marry into the management class of the St George brewery?

But about this time a group of German engineers came to the factory to install sophisticated modern machinery. Tewabé was assigned to help them. He so impressed them that they recommended him for promotion. His salary and status climbed, and this emboldened him to take the plunge.

As was customary with such affairs, he gathered together a group of his elders – in this case, senior co-workers at the brewery who were also on good terms with Mola – and he laid out his desires before them. Already impressed by his character and now also by the strength of his convictions, they agreed to form a delegation. They would convey Tewabé's formal request to Mola for an engagement with his daughter, Ayanalem.

Tewabé was twenty-seven years old; she was fourteen.

The widower Mola was already concerned that his motherless daughter was old enough to lose her virginity and thereby be ruined. With this in mind he was keen to see her married, or at least engaged, and hence prepared to listen to Tewabé's elders. But it soon became apparent that his extended family was aghast at the prospect of a family jewel being swept up in the grasp of some dusty factory-man. Surely there was a better family with which to form a liaison?

Meanwhile, Tewabé's mother, back in the countryside in Shewa, was equally unimpressed. What was the point of marrying a city girl who had no land and not even any animals? What could she bring to the table? But in this instance, Tewabé took no notice of her opinions.

Mola's extended family hurriedly presented the cases for two rival suitors, from good families of their acquaintance. His sisters, brothers and great-aunts took turns to badger him.

Everyone waited.

Finally, Mola made up his mind. Tewabé lacked social connections and prestige, but nevertheless displayed fine character, and would therefore make the best husband for his daughter.

Mola's family was dismayed. Tewabé's elders at the brewery were elated. Tewabé himself went into shock.

Oh my God! he thought. *This beautiful girl, so young, the daughter of my boss – what am I going to do with her? How will I be able to look after her like a proper husband should?*

He panicked and told the elders: 'I cannot marry her.' They, needless to say, were unimpressed.

'What are you doing to us?' they hectored. 'You make us plead to Mola on your behalf. We tell him how strong your feelings are, how strong is your resolve. Now we come back and tell you that you have won the girl and you are climbing up a tree and hiding with your pants stained brown! Do you know how embarrassed we will be if you make us go back to Mola and tell him you are not going to do anything after all? Do you know how bad it is to put us in this position?'

'Okay,' mumbled Tewabé. 'I'll do the engagement.'

Ayanalem is seated in the middle of her marital bed like a colossus, her legs spread wide on either side of her stomach. Sosina's mother's bed, day and night, is the centre of their household in Addis. All activities pivot around Ayanalem here, where she is marooned, tethered to the oxygen bottle at her bedside; where we listen to her side of the story.

'I was born in St George beer,' she starts in English — and stops. She bows her head. Everything is difficult for her now.

'Mimi,' she says to Sosina, who has this nickname, 'Mimi, translate for me.'

Ayanalem apologises for her English even though I am in her country and don't know a single word of Amharic. She understands English well enough but can speak it only slowly, painfully. When she was younger it was better. All her high school classes were in English. She learnt about the history of Ethiopia in English. She learnt about King Solomon and the Queen of Sheba and the line of Solomonic kings that stretched through the great empires of Axum and Lalibela (now tourist destinations) to the emperors Tewodros, Menelik II and finally His Excellency Haile Selassie. She learnt about the great victory over the Italians at the Battle of Adwa in 1896, and about Mussolini's revenge; all this in a foreign language.

Now she will talk in Amharic and let herself be translated.

'My father began as a storekeeper at the St George brewery. He organised the ingredients to make the beer: the grains and things.'

So this is how not only Sosina but her mother, too, grew up at the brewery.

'My father, Mola Tessema, had fifteen brothers and sisters. They all lived to be over eighty but my father died at sixty-two. He was the unlucky one,' says Ayanalem. Doubly so because his wife died even younger.

'He had to be our father and our mother,' said Ayanalem. 'My mother died when I was four. My brother was three months.'

Her breath is heavy with asthma and memories.

'My family came from Ancober. Do you know that town? It is in the countryside. They came to settle in Addis Ababa before the Italian war. There was work here for my father at the brewery.'

It is late by now. Night drops suddenly in Addis. The sun falls behind the mountains. The boy Sosina calls the Guard enters the bedroom and passes Ayanalem some rumpled notes of Ethiopian birr. She says a word or two to him in Amharic and he nods. She counts the notes and puts them in the small Tupperware container by her knee. She gives the Guard another banknote in return, the change, which he duly goes off to deliver. Ayanalem picks up an exercise book with covers folded back upon each other and writes some figures in a column she has drawn. She is the banker of the household. As well as a family home it is a hotel, restaurant and café. All financial transactions flow in and out via her Tupperware container and her exercise book. She keeps track of every birr. A couple is booking in, short stay, for Room Eleven: 50 birr. Two ladies want dinner in the restaurant: 42 birr. Amaha needs to buy petrol for his car: 200 birr.

Ayanalem takes a big wheezy breath and adjusts her position on the bed.

'I am fat,' she says sadly. 'Look at me. You would not know how beautiful I was. When I was young everyone asked me if I was a daughter of Haile Selassie. I looked just like a member of the royal family. You look at the pictures! Same nose, same eyes, same hair. Fine hair. Now – no hair! My hair is white!'

She shows Sosina and I the top of her scalp and smiles ruefully, as if to say: What can you do! This is what God brings us!

A portrait of Jesus in electric blue gleams above her bedhead. In a country where Christians and Muslims have lived side by side for centuries, Sosina's family follows the teachings of the Ethiopian Orthodox church, the country's largest religious group – and it is Ayanalem who is most devout.

She is tired now. What were we saying?

'The brewery, Mama.'

'Yes, so I grew up living at the brewery and that is where your father saw me, Mimi, because he worked there. He saw me walking by each day on my way to school and decided he would like to marry me. I was beautiful then. Fourteen years old. And he was a man.'

'Did you talk to him?'

'Oh, no! We never spoke.'

Sosina says, 'Mama, tell us how he kidnapped you.'

Ayanalem noticed they were gathering a lot of spices and making preparations at her father's house for a grand banquet, but she didn't know it was for her own engagement. She helped out in the kitchen and did all the normal work she would do for a big occasion.

It was not until a week before the party that her father asked to speak with her in private. He started crying. He told her that she was getting married. Ayanalem started crying, too. She was frightened at the thought of it. She felt like she was still a child inside a body that had changed. But her father reminded her that she was motherless and he had sole responsibility for her future. He had made up his mind that this was best.

'Tewabé is a good man,' he told her. 'He'll look after you. He won't harm you.'

Ayanalem, who couldn't live without her father's permission, steeled herself for this unknown future.

Two days before the engagement, Tewabé was ushered in to meet Ayanalem for the first time. He had borrowed money to buy her presents: fine clothes, gold earrings, a gold necklace, a gold ring. The couple-to-be exchanged a bare few words. He was a grown man, almost twice her age. All they shared was a mutual awkwardness in each other's company.

The deal agreed between Tewabé's elders and Mola was that, after the big engagement party at Mola's house had lasted for the customary several days, Tewabé would allow Ayanalem to live with her father for another two years so that she could mature and finish her studies at high school, before they married and began to live together.

After the party, at first everything went according to this plan. The engaged Tewabé and Ayanalem would cross the road to avoid each other in the street. They never spoke. Tewabé watched Ayanalem on her way to and from school as she grew older and Ayanalem tried to avoid his eye, thinking ahead to her marriage and what this strange man might expect from her.

But after a year or so Tewabé began to hear rumours from his friends in the brewery who also had connections with Mola's family. They sat with Tewabé around a table at the pub inside the St George brewery compound each (let's imagine) with a pint in front of him, and told him about the whispers they were hearing. Apparently many in Mola's family remained unhappy at the prospect of Tewabé wedding Ayanalem. A plot was being hatched, so the whispers went, to take Tewabé's engagement ring from Ayanalem's finger. A new potential husband had entered the scene, a much richer man, a government man. A government man would have the power to *take* Ayanalem.

This is the way these things worked at that time in Addis Ababa.

The government man, according to the whispers, would one day abduct her from her father's house. These things happened all the time. He would simply take Ayanalem: take her away, and take her – in the sexual sense. She would no longer be a virgin and the damage would be done.

The government man would then send his elders to inform Mola that he had taken his daughter, and the elders would negotiate for a marriage to take place. Mola would have little power but to sue the government man for taking his daughter, if he chose, but it would be too late by then to turn back what had already happened and, in any event, there was never much to be gained by suing a government man.

Tewabé's elders, each with a pint in front of him at the St George brewery pub, talking sotto voce in case of eavesdroppers, told Tewabé they'd heard whispers that the government man could be taking Ayanalem any time now. Tewabé felt his blood racing to his fingertips as he clenched the handle of his beer glass, and his cheeks grow hot with rage. Soon after he heard this story from the elders, he bought a gun.

A gun was not too hard to buy in Addis Ababa at that time, but the cost was 600 birr, which, even after Tewabé's most recent promotion, equalled four months of his salary. Tewabé had to go to a good friend of his and ask to borrow the 600 birr, while managing not to mention why he needed it.

Tewabé bought a gun because he decided that, if Ayanalem was to be kidnapped by the government man, he, Tewabé, must get in first with a kidnapping of his own. He developed a secret plan.

First, he needed to find a way to trick Mola into allowing Ayanalem to leave the house...

Now, it happened that one of Tewabé's two best men at the engagement party had lately become very ill. Tewabé pleaded with his other best man, the healthy one, to visit Mola on his behalf and ask that Ayanalem be allowed to leave the house to visit the sick best man in his hospital bed. The healthy best man went to the house, prostrated himself on the floor and kissed Mola's foot, in the customary sign of extreme respect, as he begged him to let Ayanalem leave the house for several hours. Tewabé's healthy best man promised that he would drive Ayanalem to and from her home at the St George brewery compound and be utterly responsible for her safety. Eventually, Mola agreed.

Tewabé hadn't told his best men about the gun.

The healthy best man drove Ayanalem to visit the sick best man in hospital, picking up Tewabé along the way. After the visit was over, Tewabé and some friends decided to stop off at a park and have a little party, with Ayanalem as the special guest. Ayanalem was a little scared, but the men were nice to her and respectful. They all drank tea together and ate some snacks.

Ayanalem began to be more anxious, because it was past the time that it had been arranged for her to return home to her father's house. She went and waited in the car and began to cry. Meanwhile Tewabé drank a few swigs of whiskey from a flask, to give him courage. He accosted his best man as he was about to get into the car to drive Ayanalem home. He told him about the plan of the government man, how it had put Ayanalem in imminent danger of being *taken*. Tewabé told his best man, having drunk a few swigs of whiskey, which the best man could smell on his breath (let's imagine), 'I am going to take her tonight.' He opened his eyes wide and stared at his best man to demonstrate just how serious he was. At which point the best man started crying and fell on the ground at Tewabé's feet. He begged Tewabé not to go ahead with the plan, and told him he could have no part in it because he had promised Ayanalem's father on his honour that he would deliver her back to him safe and sound.

Ayanalem was crying inside the car and panicking, saying, 'I have to go home now, my dad is going to kill me!' Shouting: 'I have to go home!'

So the two men got into the car, but not before Tewabé took one last swig of whiskey to give him courage.

(Sosina says to me, when she reads this chapter: 'I like it how this part is like a movie!')

The best man started to drive towards the St George brewery, but it wasn't very long before Tewabé, becoming increasingly agitated as he realised that this was the most important moment of his life, said to his friend: 'I want you to drive us somewhere else, not to the house of her father.'

But his friend said: 'Tewabé, you know I cannot do that. You know I have made a promise to her father.'

Ayanalem cowered in the back seat.

Tewabé looked out of the window at the dusty Addis street, with goats and donkeys swarming everywhere, and remembered once again the story of the hijackers he had recently read about in the news, hijackers who drew a gun on the pilot of an Ethiopian Airlines flight and forced him to go wherever they wanted.

He pulled out the gun from his jacket pocket and pointed it at the head of his best man.

'Jesus!' said his best man. 'What are you doing?'

Tewabé put the gun away again and said: 'Okay, I can force you to drive us wherever I want, because if you don't I will kill you and I will kill her.'

Having seen the gun, the best man was terrified, believing that Tewabé was mad enough or strong enough to carry out his threat. He offered to take Tewabé anywhere his car could travel to in Ethiopia.

Tewabé said he should take them to a big hotel that lay on the outskirts of the city, a long way from the house of Ayanalem's father. They pulled up outside the hotel and Tewabé made sure he could book a room for three nights, before he sent his best man away. Ayanalem, by this time, was almost unconscious, delirious from crying and fear.

Tewabé and Ayanalem stayed together at the hotel for three nights.

She was taken.

As soon as Mola realised that the best man of Tewabé was not about to bring his daughter home, he went crazy. He became so angry that he couldn't think, and all he wanted to do was kill Tewabé. He went out onto the street outside his house and fired his gun into the air again and again. All the men in his family, and the neighbours, too, came out with their guns and fired them into the air as well, in solidarity with Mola. They were like a band of warriors from the old days, seeking vengeance.

Mola and his family and neighbours started looking for Tewabé's house, because they wanted to murder him. They asked around at the brewery and soon found out where he lived. They went to his house, which he shared with several friends, but nobody answered the door when Mola pounded on it. Tewabé, foreseeing the likelihood of such a reaction from Ayanalem's father, had advised his friends to stay away from the house. He had even told the woman who lived there as their cook that she should disappear for a few days; go visit her family in the countryside.

Mola was quite happy to break down the door of Tewabé's house and fire his gun in all directions. He asked a person who knew Tewabé to tell him behind which door lay Tewabé's bedroom. And then he fired his gun several times straight through that door, so that if Tewabé and Ayanalem were lying inside they would have both been killed. But of course they were lying instead at the big hotel faraway on the outskirts of the city.

When Mola had done enough shooting, I imagine, to temporarily exhaust the blindness of his rage, he returned home.

Meanwhile the healthy best man of Tewabé was by this time sick with fear, since it was he who Mola would blame for letting Tewabé kidnap Ayanalem. The best man ran around to all of the elders of Tewabé to tell them what had happened, and pleaded with them to intercede once more with Mola on behalf of Tewabé. He told them that Tewabé was a good man who had only kidnapped Ayanalem to stop the rich government man from kidnapping her instead. But the elders were so angry with the best man that they didn't accept his pleas. Even when he lay down on the floor to kiss their feet they kept pushing him away. He lay down and kissed their feet again, but they pushed him away. (You know we are imagining these details. This is the timbre of the story as passed on through Sosina.)

He lay down at the feet of the elders and accepted all of the anger they dropped on him, until at last he had lain down for long enough, and they agreed to talk to Mola on behalf of Tewabé.

The next day Mola received the elders, and listened to their arguments. At first he just got angry again and wanted to take his gun, find Tewabé and shoot him; but he couldn't find out where he was – since the best man hadn't told the elders, just in case.

After many hours and several days of talking, Mola at last agreed with the elders, because he remembered that he had always believed Tewabé to be a good man and a fitting husband for his daughter. Now it was time to swallow his pride and agree that the marriage could go ahead, even if the events leading up to it had been less than ideal.

He agreed with the elders that, as was traditional after a pre-nuptial kidnapping, Ayanalem would now return home to her father's house while preparations for the grand wedding with Tewabé were completed. For, even after a girl had been taken, it was well-established that she should return home to her family for the ritual of her legal transfer to her husband, to be enacted on the wedding day. This way, everyone agreed to forget about the kidnapping and celebrate a new beginning for their son and daughter.

The best man raced to the big hotel to bring the good news to Tewabé and Ayanalem, breathless—

Tewabé said no.

No?

'I cannot trust them,' he said. 'If I give her back how do I know her family won't give her away to that government man?' And, he added dramatically, 'If they do that I will have to kill them all!'

It was hard to square this man of passion with his older self on the couch, watching Premier League soccer. But he came to life in the telling.

Tewabé's strong stand stirred his friends to lend him their support. They started turning up one by one at the hotel. They brought food and held a big party in the hotel room with Tewabé and Ayanalem.

Another big party got underway almost simultaneously at Mola's house, where the elders gathered with their own food and drink, and took turns to say to Mola: 'It's okay! After all, you already gave her to him. Why are you getting so angry? She'll be his wife now, and he'll look after her. You don't need to worry!'

Mola felt better with all of the food and drink and, in particular, the encouragement and reassurances of his trusted friends. He agreed that Tewabé could keep Ayanalem with him while he, Mola, made all of the preparations for the wedding, and that Ayanalem would come home only one day before the big day, by which time it would be too late for the government man or anyone else to kidnap her.

With everything at last agreed, Tewabé took Ayanalem back to his own house, where they could see for themselves the bullet holes and the broken doors her father had left behind. They could imagine how the bullets would have gone right through each of them in the bedroom. This was one of the first experiences they shared.

By this time, Ayanalem was no longer scared of Tewabé. He treated her well, was gentle and kind. She could foresee that her married life would not be too bad after all.

Underneath it all, Mola still found himself angry with Tewabé for the kidnapping of his daughter. In usual circumstances, the groom would be encouraged to invite forty or fifty friends and family to the wedding, which by tradition takes place at the house of the bride's parents. But Mola said Tewabé must come alone and take his bride. He could not bring his forty or fifty guests because he had broken the rules by taking Ayanalem before the wedding.

Tewabé was resigned to this arrangement, and didn't invite his mother or anyone else from his family in the countryside to the wedding. He planned to bring only three or four of his best men to support him.

The day of the wedding arrived. Ayanalem had gone home to her father's house to dress up and be made altogether beautiful and sparkling. Tewabé stepped outside his house, in his finest wedding clothes, and was surprised to discover sixty of his friends had gathered to make a special wedding procession with him. Mola had relented at the last minute.

All of Tewabé's sixty friends joined him at the house of Mola, where the priest performed the marriage ceremony and there was singing and dancing until well into the night. They ate three whole cows. No matter that half of Ayanalem's relatives were still sulking because of the lost opportunity with the government man.

Before Ayanalem had turned sixteen, her first daughter would be born. This was the beautiful one who could not do walkovers.

3

The problem of the food

Why do I want to tell Sosina's life as if a series of fables? This is how I hear it, I suppose, as *she* tells it. At the same time I write with my (white Western) self always in the mirror. So here I am, stumbling into Addis Ababa for the first time, on Sosina's invitation...

Of all of the things that, in my secret thoughts, I was not looking forward to in Addis Ababa – danger, sickness, begging, discomforting displays of poverty – I dreaded most the food.

Sosina had come back to Addis Ababa for three months, to introduce her new baby to her family. She had invited me to visit her and work on the book. I could meet her family, interview her mum and dad, get a feel for the place that made her, the place she carries with her through the streets of Melbourne. She could take me around.

I had flown from Paris, where we were lucky enough to be living for six months while I had study leave from my job as a lecturer and my wife, Linda, had long-service leave from her own job. The journey from Paris to Addis Ababa is shorter and cheaper than it is from Australia.

I booked my ticket to stay a week in Ethiopia, in early December. Sosi said to me, 'A week is hardly any time at all!' She said if I stayed longer she could take me to the countryside, from where her father came. We could see more of the sights.

'I can only afford a week away from my family,' I said. In truth, I felt that a week in Addis might be as much as I could cope with, first time around. I had a bad track record for Third World culture shock. I remembered travelling to Indonesia as a fourteen-year-old, on a Community Aid Abroad tour with my Oxfam-oriented mother. The food was so spicy that even the food they assured me was mild was *too* spicy. I got sick and had my insides peeled. Then we visited a *kretek* (clove cigarette) factory: a room with a thousand women sitting on the floor rolling clove cigarettes. I was so allergic to something (cloves?) that my eyes streamed and I had to cover my face with a handkerchief like a consumptive cowboy. Addis Ababa, I was thinking in my wimpy Western way, was going to be even more Third World–ish than Java in the late seventies.

I had, only a few months previously, laid eyes on Africa for the first time, from the southernmost tip of Spain, where we had come on a relaxing *European* family holiday from Paris. In the distance, across the water, it looked much closer than I expected.

I had scrambled up the steps to the mirador on the ramparts of Tarifa to catch the view before the sunset exhausted all its colours to the west. The Moroccan coastline was etched into the sea; rising above it, a craggy line of blue-grey mountains. They felt close enough to touch, as if I might be able to reach out and re-mould their unfixed contours with a spatula. I could see why people since prehistoric times have felt the urge to travel to the other side, by boat, makeshift raft or swimming.

'Could you swim there, Dad?' eleven-year-old Louis asked, still young enough to believe my powers might be surprisingly extensive, although he now knows that I could never have played professional football (my own realisation that extensive glory in either football or cricket was beyond my reach happened at about the same age; one of those little dreams you fold away in a pocket). No, I'm not a strong swimmer. Perhaps I could make it if I took it slowly, breast-stroking, if I didn't panic. I could stop and rest, floating on my back if I grew tired, distracting myself with clouds in place of sharks.

This strait is, they say, one of the world's most treacherous stretches of water. A bottleneck between the Mediterranean and the vast Atlantic where the ancient Romans thought Atlantis lay submerged, a narrow gap through which all the waters of the *known world* had to squeeze to mingle with the waters of the *unknown world* and be refreshed.

These days, when African asylum seekers swim across the straits, or come across in makeshift vessels, the lucky ones, it is said, are picked up by the Spanish police and placed in a detention centre near Tarifa before being shipped home again. Some float loose onto the streets of Madrid and Barcelona with no rights or documents – you can see them in the Plaça Reial in Barcelona performing acrobatic feats on the naked concrete for the tourists at the outdoor restaurants. The unlucky are found washed up on the rocks along the Spanish coast; the poor souls who couldn't drift on their backs for long enough while the cruise ships big as Gibraltar rumbled by, their port-holed dreamers sleeping off the excitement of another day spent tilting Segways back and forth through the narrow streets of Cádiz or Malaga. The unlucky are buried without ceremony in local cemeteries by Catholic priests.

Ethiopia itself has no coastline, now that Eritrea is independent. Sosina, at her primary school in Addis, looked at Australia on the map of the world in her classroom and felt sorry for it, floating so alone, far out in the ocean. *That is the first place that will sink,* she thought to herself.

On the KLM flight, about to leave Khartoum for Addis, the Dutch flight attendants were having trouble settling all the passengers in their seats.

A small group of African teenagers had joined the flight. In my ignorance, I couldn't tell if they were Ethiopian or Sudanese. The girls wore the hijab. For some reason the group had been seated separately, dotted across several rows. An older boy among them, who seemed to have taken upon himself the role of leader, moved about the cabin as if to reassure them. I was thinking: perhaps they hadn't flown before? Were they frightened to be travelling on a huge aircraft like this? Or was that a racist projection on my part?

Several of the girls kept springing from their seats to discuss things with each other. You must return to your own seats, said a flight attendant in English. You cannot sit here if it is not your proper seat.

Another flight attendant pointed out the electronic game consoles attached to each seat and the kids were happily distracted. As the plane prepared to taxi to the runway, the in-flight safety video droned through its familiar litany. The images on the screen demonstrated the use of the life jackets and the oxygen procedures.

As the plane readied for take-off, the attendants moved through the cabin for their final checks.

I saw one of them stop by the seat of one of the teenagers, across in the other aisle. The flight attendant giggled and motioned to her colleague. They were both laughing now and putting up their hands to cover their mouths, as they looked at the kids in the seats around them.

I slid up in my seat to see what all the fuss was about.

The children sat stony-faced in their seats, wearing their orange life jackets. Fully inflated.

I smiled along with the flight attendants.

On the plane I felt at home. Positively smug. But as soon as I stepped off in Addis I was lost and far away: a foreigner, *ferenji*. Kids call out the word to you on the street, but the guidebook instructs you not to pay any attention, or else they will latch on to you to try to sell you something, or take you somewhere, or in some other way take advantage of what is clearly, to them, your massive wealth and gullibility.

Addis is not a tourist town. There could hardly be a starker contrast to it than Paris – not only the greatest tourist attraction in the world but also a city famous over centuries for its unparalleled industries *de luxe*. Perfumeries, fine cabinet-makers, haute couture workshops, milliners, chocolatiers, et cetera. In Paris, a middle-class woman might spend 800 euros on a pair of boots. You would pay an Addis waitress' monthly wage for a single gourmet sausage from the Bastille market.

There were four different queues for travellers arriving at the airport from international flights. Each queue had a different purpose but, apart from the one for those who hadn't already bought their Ethiopian visas, I couldn't fathom what they were. Since I hate to lose out in a queue I rehearsed standing in one and then another, and finally the third, following the tides of travellers who seemed to know what they were doing.

Sosi had promised to meet me at the airport. I could see a pulsing mass of enthusiastic greeters waving and straining their necks in our direction, out beyond the baggage screeners. I trusted she would be somewhere in that crowd. We hadn't made a Plan B. I had no phone number or address for her. If she wasn't there I'd – I supposed I would, basically, wait. I had no desire to face the imagined wilds of Addis Ababa on my own. If I had to wait too long I could eventually find my way to a hotel and send an email, which most likely eventually she'd get (although later I found out how hard it was at that time in 2009 to even get onto the Internet in Addis).

I cleared customs and edged my suitcase out into the rapids of the arrival hall. Already here, at the country's showcase international airport, the poverty of the place was evident. Stark, featureless and chaotic, this was nothing like the glamorous shopping malls of Melbourne or Dubai, even though its basic features were familiar: anxious faces looking through me, friends and relations hugging, a row of neat men with name cards. Suddenly there she was: her shining face.

'Hi, Dave!' she said, and we embraced. 'This is my brother, Amaha.' Amaha smiled and shook my hand. He led us out into the cool air of the carpark. Overhead, a dark cloudless sky. The air dry like Perth, where I grew up.

Amaha's English, although infinitely better than my Amharic, was nonetheless basic. But his night-time driving through the streets of Addis in his battered old Corolla seemed masterful. I swear that Addis has no definite shape, no absolute geography. It has no centre and no periphery. Addis Ababa was only founded as the imperial capital as recently as 1886, by the Emperor Menelik II. For many years thereafter it was little more than a series of connected villages, stretched across an undulating plateau surrounded by gentle hills. In time these villages have stretched and merged as roads have wrapped around them, lacing them into the semblance of a city.

Maps of Addis, it seemed to me, would be of only tangential value. The greatest proportion of the streets and roads had, at that time at least, no street signs, which only reflected the deeper reality that they had no names. The address for the house of Ayanalem and Tewabé, the one that is also a hotel, restaurant and café, was as follows: 'If you are coming from the airport, drive straight to the Medhane Alem Church, the biggest church in Addis, then turn right and drive towards the big roundabout called 22 Mazoria, and once you are on the roundabout don't take the turn-off to the Children's Hospital but take the road instead towards Signal and a few hundred metres up, on the left hand side, you'll come to a gateway past the painted Pepsi sign on the wall of the café'.

Yes, the address is the same as the directions to the address.

The most vivid images of any foreign place are those that strike first, in the initial blast of strangeness. For me it is often the drive into town from the airport: the skyscraper cliffs of Manhattan lining the East River; the tides of motorbikes flowing beneath the licorice power lines of Ho Chi Minh City; the night-time road into Manila in the late eighties, arched with clouds of dust illuminating an endless procession of trucks, mini vans, fluorescent jeepneys, motorbikes, pedestrians and animals, amidst a cacophony of honking horns.

Addis was barely lit at night. There wasn't the wherewithal for flashy neons or illuminated billboards. Modest concrete buildings and smaller homemade corrugated iron dwellings lined the quiet late-evening streets. Along the rough roadsides, pedestrians, alone or in pairs, picked their way home. At intervals, in gaps between the buildings, dirt alleys and laneways could be seen disappearing into slums behind, giving the impression that the city was hollow, with the veneer of respectability that coated each major road masking a jumbled maze of deprivation.

Everything is different in Ethiopia, for the naive Westerner.

To start with, nine o'clock in the morning is called three o'clock, since the hours of the clock start from dawn, and again from sunset. Makes sense, really, especially if you're on the equator and the days hardly change all year round. Also, as I tried to explain already, any given year in my calendar is still seven years in the future, according to the calendar of an Ethiopian.

There is no divide between the metropolitan and the pastoral in Addis. In the heart of the city, a herd of goats grazed on a bare plot of land right outside the Sheraton Addis Ababa, the most splendid hotel in the country, home away from home to foreign presidents and monarchs. Not far away along the inner city roadside verges, flocks of sheep nibbled at any scrap of dirt approximating grass. Donkeys, too, were common. These are the sad-eyed utes or pick-up trucks of Addis, their curved backs bearing heavy sacks or piles of firewood.

Ethiopia has over ninety languages. Amharic, the country's dominant language, which Sosina's family speaks, has over two hundred letter variations in its distinctive alphabet, and its literature dates back centuries.

Ethiopia owes its cultural distinction to its proud independent history. From the Queen of Sheba to his maximal divinity Haile Selasse and beyond, the country was (almost) never conquered. It has been described as a natural fortress, a temperate castle surrounded by the deserts and the jungles of the tropics. Its central provinces cover a high plateau sawn through by chain after chain of ragged mountains. This topology, and its fierce defenders, deterred centuries of invaders: Arabs, Swahili, Sudanese, Somali, French and British.

Virtually alone in all of Africa (along with Liberia), Abyssinia was never colonised in the feverish and greedy late–nineteenth century European scramble – five years and a few grotesque massacres under Mussolini in the 1930s hardly counts, being merely long enough to have imported a taste for espresso and spaghetti.

Ethiopian food, too, apart from the minor inroads made by the aforementioned Italianate pasta and espresso, and a few pastries, has yet to be colonised. This, to my mind, was all to the good – in theory.

The Corolla motored through the night. At a major intersection stood a giant ship of flapping blue: one of the many new buildings under construction in Addis at building sites advertising new hotels or luxury condos. This one, a concrete shell ten or so storeys high and encased in scaffolding, was entirely wrapped in blue plastic sheeting. The plastic had torn loose every few metres, giving the impression of a thousand sails on a cubic-square rigger.

Abruptly, just beyond this building, we turned off onto a side road through a higgledy-piggledy rank of ancient East Berlin-esque taxis. This road was wide but so rough and uneven that the car couldn't move faster than a walking pace.

'This is the street of my mum and dad,' said Sosi.

As we bumped violently along the dusty road I saw, over the space of a few hundred metres, high fences topped with barbed wire, tiny roadside shops no bigger than holes in a wall, a rundown video-rental store, the plastic-spangled doorway of a local bar, an unmarked wood yard where long eucalypt saplings were stripped and sharpened and stacked for sale as posts, a filthy open sewer and, next to this, perched against a fence, a makeshift dwelling of wood and tin no bigger than a cupboard, made as if it were the least space in the world that any home could occupy.

The residents had respectfully asked the government to pave the street, Sosi told me. The government told the residents they would have to pay 30 per cent themselves. The residents had raised the money but were still waiting on the government. They didn't know when it would happen; one day, maybe...

The black night in Addis Ababa was alive with the deep-brown faces and bodies of the locals. We bumped along in our tin cocoon, making feeble headway, as if rowing into a howling gale through choppy waves. I was the *ferenji* in the front seat. I felt as if I glowed like something in a shop window. I could tell already from the way people looked at me at the airport that my paleness, my height, made me a freak. Sosi said I should be careful taking out my iPhone in public because it would be stolen. In my pocket it felt like a bar of gold.

A young man stepped out from the doorway of what looked like a tiny bar. He veered toward our slowly moving vehicle.

'Sosina – Mimi!' he called. 'Where are my new jeans?' he asked her in Amharic.

Amaha paused the car, mid-pothole.

'I brought you new shoes already, Ayele!' she said. 'You are not going to get any new jeans yet. Keep going, Amaha.'

And again, out the window to the young man, as we edged away: 'No, you have to stop drinking. If you get yourself together, maybe I'll bring you some new jeans.'

'Oh, Sosina, but you promised! Wait, wait!'

'I promised you the shoes, Ayele,' she said. She shook her head at me and rolled her eyes.

'That guy, Ayele, he is a nice guy, but he drinks too much now. He lives here in our street. I know him from when I was young. I always try to help him a little bit: each time I come back to Addis I bring him something from Australia, but now every time he asks for more. I'm not just going to give him more.'

Amaha kept his eyes on the road ahead.

We arrived at the gateway just beyond the hand-drawn Pepsi sign on the wall, and Amaha tooted the horn. The Guard opened the gate for us to drive in. He closed the gate behind us and we were safe inside the compound of the house of Sosina's parents.

'Are you hungry, Dave?' asked Sosi.

I had tasted Ethiopian food in Melbourne once and was pretty sure I didn't like it. It's not that I'm a *particularly* fussy eater – I've grown out of that, I hope – but let's just say I'm not always at my bravest when it comes to trying new culinary sensations.

Also, I am thin and need food often. A week is not a long time, but in this context not a short time either.

Thinking of this issue in advance, I had sought the advice of an Australian circus friend who had travelled previously to Addis to visit Sosina's family. He recommended importing a secret stash of muesli bars to return to, in the comfort of my bedroom, for sustenance and solace, 'after another hard day of pretending to eat *injera*'.

Injera was always going to be the chief stumbling block I faced – it's the national staple of Ethiopia, a wide, flat air-pocked bread, which in my memory looked and tasted like a thin, bitter, raw crumpet, realised on a massive scale. In a typical Ethiopian meal *injera* will be all of plate, utensil and staple ingredient. A single shared-platter dish will be lined with *injera*, atop which various dollops of spicy *wat* (a meat or vegetable sauce) will be dotted around, possibly interspersed with salads. To eat, you tear a piece from the *injera* closest to you and use it as a kind of sponge to pinch and mop up a mouthful of *wat* or salad.

Breakfast, lunch and dinner.

Sosina, ever-mindful and considerate with her Western friends, took pains to ease me in slowly. The night I arrived from the airport, she gave me a supper of post-Mussolini spaghetti, with the most delicious, jammy fresh tomato sauce I had ever tasted.

The *injera* only made its first appearance at breakfast the next day. It didn't seem as bitter as expected. Perhaps this is because it was truly authentic *injera*, more easily found in Ethiopia, being made from a grain called *teff* endemic to the country. *Teff* grains, apparently, are extremely fine and therefore difficult to process; they are considered unlikely to catch on in other places.

I ate *injera* with scrambled eggs and dhal for breakfast. I ate *injera* with vegetarian *wat* and salad for lunch; and with the special delicacy of fresh chicken *wat* for dinner. Despite myself, and my muesli bars, I found something very strange occurring. I was developing a deep fondness for *injera* and all of its accompaniments. At every meal we ate, Sosina and I alone in the dining room, joined occasionally by Tewabé – Ayanalem could eat little, but what she did eat she ate upon her bed, and the dining habits of everyone else in the household was a mystery – my respect grew for the genius of the 'chef'. After all, the kitchen the chef worked in had no sink or stove. It was, at first sight, dark and gloomy, bare and poor. On the floor in one corner stood four or five freestanding gas burners on which all cooking operations were performed. Elsewhere on the floor were places to chop things up, a shelf or two for spices. Washing up happened at a back-breaking tap out in the small courtyard. A refrigerator on the verandah was barely used, except for storing beer and newly slaughtered meat. It would be hard work to cook in such a kitchen. But everything was painstakingly clean, and the food as fresh as could be found anywhere.

'You should not eat any salads in Addis,' Sosina told me firmly. 'Your body won't be used to it; you might get sick.'

'Well, what about here at home? Didn't we have salad last night?'

'No problem. Here, it's fine. Everything is fresh. You can eat anything and not get sick.' She said it as if there was nothing surer in the world, and I believed her.

'I know,' she said, 'how the chef prepares all of the food. She has a special way to do everything. For instance, when she washes the salad, she puts the tiniest amount of detergent in the water.'

I trusted Sosina. I couldn't taste the detergent.

And I must say that I have never felt better than after a week of eating Ethiopian food at the house of Ayanalem and Tewabé.

Sosi had to deal with her own food problems in coming home to Addis. Ayanalem's bedroom was stacked with the tins of formula Sosi had imported from Australia for her baby, Raeey, because she couldn't be assured of finding the same quality of formula in Addis. She had to ship in an electric kettle to boil the water, too, not to mention disposable nappies by the carton.

Raeey would often be the centre of attention in Ayanalem's bedroom, lying or sitting or rolling on the special rug that Sosi had stretched out on the tiled floor for her, or playing with the plastic toys Sosi had brought from Australia, attended by whichever of Sosi's five girl-cousins from the country did not have to be at school or doing chores and had managed to inveigle her way into the plum role of Raeey's entertainer. Ayanalem would watch in delight and sing her favourite nursery rhymes to the pampered baby until, inevitably, another guest would arrive, bringing news from the city or the countryside, and, the chef's assistant would arrange the dried grass, incense and ornamental tray of the traditional coffee ceremony that greets each visitor, and pour out a tray full of small strong black coffees for all to share.

Importing the formula and nappies was, like many endeavours, not an easy task, as I saw when Sosi took me to the airfreight terminal one day. Her box from Melbourne had arrived. Down a long road at the back of the airport, armed guards made us step out of Amaha's car and show our passports. Amaha and Sosi had been here many times before. 'I'm sorry, Dave,' she said, 'This might take a while. Now you're seeing the real life in our country.'

A wide loading bay backed on to the carpark. At one end, a crowd of people milled in front of a high mesh fence, behind which everybody's treasures were laid out in a labyrinth. A concrete walkway led away to a series of offices for bureaucrats and freighting companies, and a large waiting room with rows of seats facing a line of counters. This is where the required paper-stamping happened. While Sosi queued up, I offered to shout Amaha a drink in the café next to the waiting room. A place unloved and disconsolate, there was scarcely anything to buy there. Coke, or a single row of donuts in a glass cabinet.

After we had spent as much time as we could bear chewing on a donut and watching MTV in the café, Amaha and I returned to find Sosina where we left her in the waiting room. 'They will want to argue with me,' she said, 'They will want to know why I am bringing so many nappies and so much baby formula to Ethiopia. They will tell me that I am going to sell them or open up a shop, in which case I should be paying taxes on them. I will already be paying enough taxes!'

Sure enough, eventually, they did argue with her, and she argued back (of course) and argued some more until (eventually) they stamped her papers and she paid her tax and could join the milling crowd waiting to be called. Amaha and I loped around on the edges. To one side perched a couple of opportunistic vendors with fold-up tables and stools, selling chewing gum and cigarettes. I was the only non-Ethiopian in sight, this not being an experience usually encouraged for or required of Western visitors or expatriates.

Finally, a man with a clipboard called out Sosi's name and perused her paperwork. She filed in to locate her barrel.

'Tip every item out for cross-checking! Count each nappy!'

She said, 'What does it matter how many there are, whether it is 302 or 305 or 412?'

And sure enough the man said, 'Well, if it's too many, it means you are going to sell them or set up a shop.'

She said, 'They are for my baby! I'm visiting here for three months and I need a lot of nappies. I'm not going to count them; it's ridiculous.'

Eventually they gave in and let her cram all the nappies and formula and other items back into the barrel. They signed the papers, yet again, opened up the big gates and wheeled the barrel over to the Corolla.

'I'm sorry, Dave,' said Sosi, 'It always takes time. You'll see; everything takes time.'

And back we were again at the front gate of the house.

4

Where passion takes you

If we cast our minds back, we might ask: why did the cigarette seller want to sell cigarettes, in the first place?

The answer is that she, Sosina, was a very expensive child.

She wanted to do many things, but her parents had six children and couldn't pay for everything. She had friends who were rich and she saw them eating ice creams, drinking *espris*. But she didn't want to ask her parents for their money.

Most of all, Sosina needed money to go to gymnastics lessons. You can imagine why the cigarette seller liked gymnastics. She first got the idea from the television in her lounge room.

Her grandmother, who came from the country, thought that all the people who appeared on the television were *in* the television, and she liked to put a cloth over it to protect herself from any of them escaping. But Sosina, who was seven years old and didn't consider things in the same way, waited for the time to come around once a week (7 pm, Friday, to be precise) when the German variety show she loved would be beamed across Ethiopia.

In preparation for the show, she would move all the couches and chairs back against the walls to make a space in the middle to perform. The whole family would sit around and watch: her very first circus performances. Sosina was impressed with every aspect of that German variety show. The costumes, the make-up, the thick black curtains, the fairy lights that dimmed and brightened. Each new element was *wow!* Serious magicians swirled around in black tails, producing birds from top hats, pouring playing cards like liquid. Girls in high-cut leotards with blonde curly hair smiled as knives sailed past their ears, and built impossible towers of flimsy platforms stacked on glasses stacked on platforms stacked on glasses stacked – up which they would climb to balance upside down on one hand. A handsome muscleman walked on his hands, strolling upside-down all the way down a staircase and up again.

Easiest to imitate, for Sosina, were the contortionists. Lying on the lounge room floor she found that she could mirror them step by step. She could bend her legs around behind her back until her toes came to rest beside her chin. That shape was called a 'zero', she declared. If she pushed her legs out even further beyond her nose the shape became a 'nine'.

'And this one is the cat,' she said. 'This one is the dog.' Sosi performed in duet with the television and her assembled family laughed and applauded. The power to produce applause is every performer's dream and narcotic. Sosina first became addicted in her parents' lounge room.

She wasted no time in taking her developing repertoire on the road – meaning, to the school playground. There, she soon learnt how to gather a crowd. She could bend. She could do the splits. She could put her leg up in the air behind her ear. She left open a mystery as to what she *couldn't* do, and this attracted a healthy respect and more applause.

Sosina had never heard of anything happening in Ethiopia remotely similar to the German variety show, although much later she found out about the acrobatics certain tribes perform at funerals, and about other traditional feats. But one day she came across a different show on the television, a kids' show with a story about children doing a gymnastics program in Addis Ababa only one hour's walk away from her house. She knew she wanted to be there.

She, who never told her father about her cigarette selling, judged that in the case of gymnastics it was also better to enrol without bothering him with the news. There was always the possibility that he might feel he should stop her from doing what she wanted, for some reason or another. The longer she waited before telling him, the more strength she would build up to negotiate.

He was too busy with his work to notice, anyway. He was too busy with his work to devote proper attention to any of his children. Like many men, he would afterwards regret this.

Sosina approached the man called Abebe who washed the training costumes for the St George football club, and asked if one day he would take her to the gymnastics centre. It was summer holidays; she could do their summer course. But if she turned up unannounced, all by herself, a scrawny little kid, they would surely be suspicious. She pleaded and pestered until he agreed. They walked there together, all the way in the hot sun up the hill, since he couldn't afford transportation. Sosina skipped along, looking like a boy with her short afro and her miniature version of the St George football team outfit: red shorts and a yellow T-shirt with a red V.

When they arrived at the YMCA club where the gymnastics classes happened, they were greeted with: 'What do you want?'

Abebe said: 'She's talented; she wants to learn from you.'

The trainer said to Sosina, 'Show us something,' and all of the other kids gathered around to watch this scrawny punk.

Sosina said: 'What do you want? A zero or a nine? Do you want cat? Do you want dog?' But, since these were names that she had invented, nobody had any idea what she was talking about.

'Just show us something,' repeated the trainer.

So Sosina started at the top and ran through her entire show list, bending bending bending, until they said, 'Oh my God, where did you learn this?' and she said, 'At home in my lounge room in front of that German variety show,' and they said, 'Okay, she can stay,' and Abebe waited patiently under the shade of a tree until it was time to accompany the performer home again.

After that, to make her own way to gymnastics three times a week, Sosina jumped in a mini-van taxi on the main road, where, being so small and jumbled up with all the other passengers, she was never made to pay.

Meanwhile: 'She's at a friend's house,' everyone would tell her father, Tewabé, if he asked. It was a communal life, with the children always at somebody's house or, if not, somebody else's. Ayanalem knew about Sosina's gymnastics classes but she too found a way to forget to tell her husband, just in case he felt he really should, as the father of the house, create a problem.

'I saw your daughter in a taxi,' a friend remarked to him one day.

'I saw your daughter walking on the street near the taxi rank,' commented another friend in passing.

'No, that wasn't her,' Tewabé told them. 'You must have seen someone else. That wasn't my daughter, Sosina. She was at somebody's house that day.'

Life continued on like this, with Sosina spending longer and longer each Saturday at gymnastics, lingering afterwards with her friends in the yard to practise flips and dancing routines, until the morning Tewabé received an official letter from the Gymnastics Federation inviting him to see his daughter performing at a festival.

After the initial shock had worn off, Tewabé asked permission from his bosses at the St George brewery to take time off work that day and go to watch his daughter perform at the festival. He was impressed with what she could do in gymnastics. Her little body was strong and supple, and she was fearless. After that, he got right behind her training. She entered the national gymnastics championship and won a trophy.

Tewabé cried.

I want to give a picture of the house of Ayanalem and Tewabé, which is also a homemade hotel, restaurant and café, the home they built after he retired from the St George brewery; because this, too, is a testament to passion.

The first thing that strikes the visitor is that no house is immediately apparent. You must imagine a property the size of an average Australian suburban block, bounded on all four sides by a high wall or fence. Then imagine that built against every part of this wall or fence, except for the double gates that open onto the unpaved road and the mysterious chaos of Addis Ababa beyond, is some structure or another, more or less modest, and that in the middle of these structures is a large red-dirt courtyard occupied with washing lines, Amaha's car, the cars of hotel guests, the family dogs and the rooster that Ayanalem has forbidden anyone to slaughter, because she has a soft spot for it. The young man they call the Guard is often to be found in the courtyard, too, when he has nothing better to do, relaxing on a chair near the front gate, playing with his third-hand mobile phone.

Each household member and guest must crisscross the plain red-dirt courtyard to walk from the café to the house, the house to the restaurant, the restaurant to the hotel, and any other perambulatory permutation. Roughly speaking, each building began life in one corner of the property but, as time has gone on, the arrangement has got more complicated. A row of extra hotel rooms has slipped in along the wall between the café and the house. A tin shed has sprung up in front of the house, and then two or three more of varying size and shape, which together shield it from the main courtyard and form a smaller concrete-floored courtyard (the latter space, as I would discover, just large enough to kill a sheep in).

If it is hard to get a bearing on where the buildings start and end, you have to remember that there have been no architects employed here, no builders, not even any plumbers, carpenters or electricians. Any one of these would be an outlandish luxury. Tewabé has built every centimetre of this establishment, installed every brick, wire and fitting. With the help of his extended family, he has drawn all of the plans and carried out all of the work, with whatever means at his disposal.

You will have a picture in your mind of what a hotel is. A hotel has a foyer or a lobby; usually elevators. If it's more fancy, it will have a pool, a gym, et cetera.

The hotel of Tewabé and Ayanalem is much more modest. It didn't even have a sign, when I first visited, that said: 'Hotel' (I later discovered its official name is 'Family Hotel'). You would only know it existed, behind that high gate, if you asked around.

There is no hotel reception or office (in case you were imagining such a thing). Guests negotiate at the front gate with the Guard, or with Amaha who manages the café. Payment is in cash, and in advance. The money and the details come to Ayanalem, sitting on her bed, or perhaps on her chair if her poor feet are being washed and massaged. She puts the money in her Tupperware container, returns change, if necessary, and makes a note of the transaction in her book.

The hotel would enjoy much better business if the road were ever paved. Suddenly a glorified country lane would become an important city thoroughfare. It would be worth building a decent hotel block, with signage. The same goes, but even more so, for the restaurant. The restaurant sports a curved wood-panelled bar below a mirrored ceiling, funky metal chairs with green-mar-bled laminex seats, and a verdant shaded patio. It is altogether charming, and a very pleasant place to spend a cool evening or a sunny morning, but nonetheless thinly patronised. Trade is sleepy. There might be a quiet couple at a table to the side, but usually that's about it. I never saw anyone sitting at the bar on the natty green-and-yellow barstools.

The café, taking advantage of its position by the roadside, the lure of an espresso machine and a glass counter lined with pastries, is livelier. You get the feeling this is the centre of Amaha's social scene, as regulars drop by.

In the café each morning, a tall, thin man occupies the table in the corner underneath the television. His beard clipped short, his back erect, he sips a free café latté and talks, but not in a way that anyone can understand. He gazes ahead into an impenetrable forest of ghosts and machinations. He is broken, and cannot be unbroken. Ayanalem has spent many years trying. This is her brother, Tamrat, the one who went to the Eritrean war, and came back with it inside him. Just like, they say, my dad did with his own war in the 1940s. My dad came back to fifteen years of hospitals, psychiatrists and experimental treatments, the sum of which was a failure. In Addis, Ayanalem's brother has a chair to sit on in the café and a tiny stool to perch on in the courtyard closer to the house. He is fed and looked after. But they can offer him no treatment, experimental or otherwise. In Australia, we used to people our yards with stone creatures, gnomes and pink flamingoes. In Addis, the yards are peopled with living ghosts.

A list of how many people, not counting the hotel guests, live squeezed together at the house of Ayanalem and Tewabé:
(The number is somewhere between twelve and fifteen.)
Ayanalem.
Tewabé.

Their second son, Amaha, who runs the café and the Corolla, takes his mother to her never-ending round of medical appointments, exchanges empty oxygen bottles for full ones.

The five young girls from the countryside – Tewabé's relatives – brought to the city by Ayanalem so they can attend high school; in exchange, they work around the house, the hotel and the restaurant, and sleep in a tiny bunkroom on the verandah.

The chef, as Sosi calls her: Emuye. The slightest woman you would ever see, with a grinning mouth of jumbled teeth. A Muslim woman from a poor background, chef in the family for eleven years, producer of a faultless supply of fresh-cooked food, with the help of…

The chef's assistant. Another young girl, perhaps even younger than the five. Not family, per se. A girl from the local area whom Ayanalem is helping out.

Another female domestic worker, whom I learnt to distinguish from the five girls only by the relative plainness of her clothes, her more sallow cheeks.

The Guard.

Another male employee, the one who helps to kill the sheep.

Ayanalem's brother, Tamrat, who went to war and is now forever broken.

Plus, for three months, Sosina and her baby girl, Raeey.

Plus, for one week, me.

Another list: those who don't live at the house of Ayanalem and Tewabé, but visit constantly. Impossible to calculate, but they include:

Tewabé's cousin, who lives around the corner, and comes for every meal. His is another sad story for Ayanalem: he suffers with an incurable degenerative disease.

Mame, the lady who each week brings fresh cheese and yoghurt from the countryside to sell to Ayanalem.

Gazahin, Tewabé's old friend, who lives across the street and let Sosina as a child teach herself to type using the typewriter in his office.

Sosina's elder sister, Israel, the beautiful one, who, unlike Sosina, only ever wanted to get married, have children and settle down in Addis. All of which she has done. She brings beautiful flower arrangements from the shop she runs, and her little girl presents hand-drawn greeting cards written in her best English for her fabled Auntie Sos.

The next-door neighbor, a nurse Sosi calls Sister, who pops in as a friend to check on Ayanalem's health every day.

The local slaughterman. (Any meat they eat is slaughtered on site, since refrigeration can't be trusted.)

The bread and butter of the hotel of Tewabé and Ayanalem are not tourists, travellers or workingmen. Occasionally, guests come into town from afar. A local NGO might take a room for several months to accommodate a visiting worker from the country. But the bread and butter of the hotel is love.

Local love.

Young love.

This is where you come when you are young and need some privacy for love in Addis Ababa. There are such places dotted around in every district of the capital.

For couples that are not yet married, the love hotel is their sanctuary. They can't afford cars to make out in – in any event, there is nowhere they could go in a car where they would not fear to be arrested. They certainly can't go home together to their parents' houses.

For the young who are employed, bringing in some money, the love hotel becomes an attractive option. Rooms – basic, clean and cheap, with a bed, a chair, a mirror and, for a premium, a bathroom with a toilet and a shower – are available on a sliding timescale. A short stay is the cheapest. This is four hours, during daylight: 25 birr showerless, 35 birr with a cold shower, 50 hot. In and out, you might say. Beyond this comes a short overnight, which is a full night and nothing more: 55 to 110 birr, depending on your shower choice. A long overnight means you can stay a full day and a night. For such lingering decadence and a hot shower, 140 birr.

From my room (hot shower), which contained a single bed, a kitchen chair, a light bulb and a very small mirror, and lay at the end of an open corridor behind the carport and the wardrobes for the linen, I could hear couples coming and going at all hours. They were quiet and respectful. Discreet. Sometimes, usually in the morning, I would wake to hear the ardent sounds of love wafting through the high glassless window in the wall between my neighbours' bathroom and my own.

There was rarely any trouble at the hotel, said Tewabé. If there was any sound of violence in the night he would go out with his gun and calm things down, evict the trouble-maker if he must. (He still has a gun!? I try to imagine this quiet man pulling out a gun from some secret hiding-place and all I can think of is how ridiculously heavy it must be.)

After a day or so, Sosina began to show me around the town; she wanted me to see her childhood haunts, beginning with the St George brewery.

I was very keen, after all this talk of the St George brewery, to visit it for myself.

I would not be disappointed.

Amaha, Sosina's almost ever-reliable brother, escorted us to St George, as the sun slid towards Sudan one afternoon. The place was packed. The entrance to the brewery compound, where Sosi's house used to be, had been subsumed by the expansion of the pub, now spread across a series of large open halls. The halls, as far as the eye could see, were filled with tables, chairs and benches occupied by groups of men drinking St George beer from identical glass tankards. The men were of all ages and the atmosphere lively but peaceful; noticeably absent were the blaring sport screens and calls to commerce of an Australian pub. The drinkers seemed to nurse their drinks over conversation rather than slosh them down. As my eye adjusted to the scene, I noticed a few women dotted here and there, also drinking St George beer out of tankards.

This pub operated with a purity of purpose and an efficiency that I had never before witnessed. A man in a glass booth sold beer tokens. Two men at beer taps poured glasses of St George draught beer. Non-stop. Three or four women handed the beers to customers in exchange for tokens, while another clutch of women swept the halls for empties, gathering up five or six in each hand, and gliding them to the washer-uppers. You could buy St George draught beer. Nothing else. What more could you want? On a warm weekend afternoon, with some time on your hands, a few old friends and the sunlight streaming in, what could possibly be finer?

Sosi hailed the passing workers who knew her from when she was a child selling cigarettes out the front. 'This one, he's the manager now; he used to be one of those boys out on the street trying to do business washing cars. Drink up, Dave. Here's another beer. They're giving us free ones.'

The more Amaha and I drank, the more that grinning at each other became a perfectly adequate form of communication, especially supplemented with a few glass-clinks.

Should we go across the road for another pub experience? we asked ourselves. *Why not?*

The pub opposite was packed, too, but slightly more up-market. A long room filled with tables, a curved bar at one end. We wandered around, trying to find an empty table. The best we could do was some spare seats at a booth where two young women sat. The young women were gracious, friendly. It struck me as refreshing to see two women like that in Addis, free to enjoy their own company, drinking together at a pub. I felt as if this overwhelmingly strange city, where I had expected women's lives to be confined by circumstance and convention, was perhaps more like Melbourne than I had imagined. They could be two young professionals out on a Friday night. The one opposite me was strikingly attractive, with huge brown eyes and an infectious smile.

We struck up a conversation with the women. The beautiful one spoke a little English. What did they do for a living? The one next to me had an office job; the beautiful one was studying English.

Amaha nudged me. He pointed at the teeth of the beautiful girl. She had a wide gap between her two front teeth. Amaha and the girl started joking together. He told the girl he had a theory: a gap between a girl's front teeth means she knows how to enjoy herself in bed. Everyone laughed with the beer. The girl gleamed at me and I started to imagine Amaha's theory might have some merit.

I joked with Amaha: 'How about your girlfriend? Does she have a gap between her front teeth?'

'Yes!' He said. 'All of my girlfriends have had a gap between their front teeth!' He beamed with the memory of the years of unabashed pleasure he'd shared with these women.

Sosi laughed and rolled her eyes.

'Do you have a boyfriend?' she asked the beautiful girl.

'I had a boyfriend,' the girl said, 'but he has gone home now to his country. Holland.'

She pulled out a photograph to show us her ex – a decidedly non-beautiful white guy.

She took off her cardigan. Her shirt fell open a little, to reveal her lacy blue bra.

'Was he nice?' I asked her, thinking of how non-beautiful he looked.

'Yes, he was nice; he was kind,' she said. 'I like foreign men,' she said. And she looked into me with her enormous eyes and sexy teeth and shirt ajar.

I started to grasp what was happening.

She – so very beautiful, so full of life – was offering herself up to me, a fantasy white guy with, as she knew, money in my pocket. She could be my African mistress and I could be her sugar daddy. I could drag her from her wretched impoverished existence, help her support her family. My own fantasies of innocent sexual attraction based on an equality of power evaporated. She was offering me her eyes, her breasts, the gap between her front teeth, whatever turned me on, if I would only give her what she needed to live on. And it would be so cheap for me to do it, so affordable. Twenty dollars for her would be a fortune – it would hardly feel like prostitution; more like charity.

Later, Sosi said to me, 'There are many, many girls like her on the streets of Addis, working in their different ways. They don't stand out unless you know what you are looking at. It is one of the only options for a young woman without a good education or connections.' This was an option she herself had been determined to escape from.

After one or two beers, we took our leave of the two women. On the way out the owner of the bar stopped us and proposed to me a business partnership exporting organic pork to Australia.

My eyes lit up. 'Why not?' I said. I imagined myself for a moment as a successful entrepreneur marketing niche Ethiopian products.

Sosi deadpanned: 'Dave, Australia has a lot of meat already; imports can't compete.' Of course she was right. I had obviously drunk more beer than I had thought. I looked back for a last glimpse of the women, but they had vanished.

One time when she was a child, a friend at gymnastics told Sosina that a circus had been started especially for children in Addis Ababa. A man called Marc LaChance who had come from Canada to teach English at the American School in Addis was behind it. One day, the story goes, Marc LaChance, driving home, saw a group of children playing acrobatic games in the street and had the idea there and then to start a circus for them. It was only much, much later that people began to say that Marc LaChance might have had other things on his mind as well, when he thought of helping little children.

The friend at gymnastics whispered to Sosina that two other children from their gym class had secretly joined this circus begun by Marc LaChance. The children didn't want to let their gymnastics teachers know in case they worried, with good cause, that all of their best students would leave to join the circus.

Sosina made up her mind: she needed to see this circus for herself. One afternoon she travelled there with her friend. It was a long way from where they lived, in the foothills above the road that passes by the massive compounds of the British and Israeli embassies. A laneway winds up a hill behind some houses to a little clearing, at the back of which stands a simple wooden building with a verandah.

One group of kids was training tumbling runs, on a mat lain on rough concrete in the yard. Another group was learning how to juggle, with small rocks. Sosina spied the tiniest little sound system.

Heaven!

She wanted more than anything in the world to join this circus.

It cost 2 birr for transport there and back to training, five afternoons a week after school. Sosina told the circus trainers that she could only come three afternoons a week, because on the other days she had to stay home and make money selling cigarettes. But it didn't take very long for Sosina to fall in love with the circus.

All the worst fears of the gymnastics teachers eventuated: one by one, their best students quit because the circus was more fun.

The circus started to do free outdoor shows. They inherited a bigger sound system and old costumes from a rich Canadian circus, to which Marc LaChance had written, asking for assistance. Every Thursday afternoon they performed what Sosi calls a 'music show', and all the local kids would come to listen. Meanwhile, a small group would go out across the city in a van to scout for a suitable place for the circus to perform the coming Sunday, such as a bare sandy football field – the only type of football field in Addis outside the rainy season. On Sundays they would borrow a truck from the Red Cross to transport the equipment, and the children would pile into a couple of minibuses. As soon as the truck arrived, they would set up the sound system with a generator, and blast out music, loud and funky. Michael Jackson or a favourite Ethiopian pop hero. Soon three or four thousand locals would gather as an audience.

The show would leap into life, every time a little better, stronger, more spectacular. For the audiences this was something new: raw local talent in their community. Every show was more or less a party. Only after all the gear was packed away again – the musical equipment, costumes, tumbling mats and juggling sticks – could the ravenous children sit down on the football field and eat the meal provided by the circus. Later, Sosina and her closest circus friends, still basking in the excitement of the show, might kick on to a bakery or café and splurge on baklava. When the sudden darkness of Addis fell, they would leap onto the mini-van taxis, dispersing for home and sleep and circus dreams.

Only a few months after joining the circus Sosina gave up cigarette selling once and for all, to train at the circus every afternoon. She was hooked.

5

Ghosts and emperors

Sosina is a professional contortionist. She can juggle up to eight balls simultaneously, bouncing them on a board of marble. She has performed to rapturous applause on Broadway in New York, at the famous Sadler's Wells theatre in London, the Sydney Opera House. And these aren't her most special attributes. She is courageous and determined; but every circus performer learns to hold the risk of death in the corners of their vision. Her best tricks are those that take much longer to perform.

For anyone who grows up in Addis Ababa outside of the elite, the biggest trick is to find a way to make a better life. For Sosina, this is the easy part; she can do anything she has to. She could go back in an instant to selling cigarettes one by one on the street. But to help her mother, brothers, sisters, cousins, and all the young kids now at Circus Ethiopia, to make a better life is not so easy. There are many things stacked against them.

As for her brother Abraham, who was exiled in Cairo for six years as a political refugee from Ethiopia, waiting for resettlement, losing hope: he is the shadow in this story, beneath Sosina's breath. He almost made it. She worked so long on that act. Together they came so close.

Will we be able to visit the cemetery in Addis? I ask her. I want to do this just as much for my sake as for hers – through the thread of suicide in our families we share a bond.

'Maybe,' she says. 'I'll think about it. I went there last time I was here. It was hard.'

We don't speak of it again that week.

One day Abraham's name, just his name, comes up with Ayanalem, sitting on her bed. She starts to cry. Sosi changes the subject. It is too soon, too hard.

Instead, Sosina takes me out into the streets of Addis. We will look for her past, her culture: the contradictions she negotiates.

We begin at a wide boulevard so important it even has a name: Churchill Street, after Winston, esteemed wartime ally of Emperor Haile Selasse.

The end of Churchill Street is in the area known as the Piazza, a hill on which a few old deco buildings, constructed by the Italians, congregate. We set off down the slope towards the Sheraton, where Sosi has bought a three-month pass to use the swimming pool. For such a celebrated road, its shabbiness at the edges is surprising. Amid a pile of boulders and rubbish squat a group of small boys wearing rags. They tend a little fire, working on extracting and cooking scraps of bright-red flesh from a pile of animal carcasses.

I have learnt to inure myself to such sights of desperation. I turned away from the man lying on the road near the sprawling marketplace of Mercato whose foot looked like it had been grafted from an elephant. 'Don't give anything to the beggars,' Sosi told me. 'You must ignore them or you'll only encourage more.'

But she stops and walks over to these boys. She asks them what they are doing; they tell her they are cooking the meat left behind on carcasses discarded by the local butchers. She gives them a 10 birr note to share. She makes this distinction: these street-boys are doing something for themselves, not begging. They can take the 10 birr and buy themselves some bread to enjoy with their meat.

Sosina is, by definition, in returning from Australia, rich in Ethiopia. She accepts the responsibility of these choices every day.

Further down Churchill Street, a small strip of tacky tourist craft shops curls around a corner. At a roundabout nearby, processions of old and battered cars and trucks, puffing out clouds of smoke, encircle one of Addis' civic monuments: the great cannon of the Emperor Tewodros.

Tewodros is famed for uniting the fractious principalities of Ethiopia under his majestic reign, back in the 1860s. As was customary at that time, his court, for reasons both political and environmental, was always on the move. Every year, once the rains had stopped, he led his army from province to province to quell the local insurrections that had sprung up in the off-season. His capital was wherever he and his 50,000-odd soldiers and camp followers chose to stop. For food, they ravaged the local crops and animals; for entertainment, they raped the women. When there was no longer sufficient food in the district to support them, they moved on again.

Tewodros faced threats from foreign powers, too: the Europeans, who were as usual eyeing off Africa for its riches. He was well aware of the technological advantages the Europeans held. He sought political and military advice from local Europeans – missionaries, envoys, adventurers – whomsoever he could trust and some he couldn't.

Superior firearms became his passion. The British and the French, wanting to leave their own imperial options open, refused to supply him with modern weapons. Instead, he turned to a small band of Swiss missionaries living on a mountain near the town of Gondar. They had some skills in smithing, did they not? He commissioned them to make for him a gun, the stupendous size of which would intimidate any enemy who heard of it.

After many years of trying, and several more or less successful prototypes, the Swiss of Gondar finally produced the greatest gun of all. Tewodros named the cannon Sevastopol, after a great battle of the Crimean War. It was in fact dubious in reliability and poor in accuracy, but fearsome in appearance.

It is said that Tewodros, in his last years, became somewhat unhinged, prone to rash decisions and impulsive massacres. His supporters and his power base dwindled, and he unwisely provoked the British by imprisoning several of their officials on his last redoubt atop the flat-topped Mount Magdala. He made his soldiers carve a road 100 kilometres long, across sheer ravines and ranges, solely so as to drag and push the unwieldy Sevastopol towards the mountain. None of his enemies dared attack him while the cannon was by his side.

But, in the end, his engineers failed him and he had to leave Sevastopol just below the summit plateau of Magdala. A massive British force led by General Sir Robert Napier charged up the other side, and Tewodros, refusing to negotiate or be captured, shot himself with a revolver which, somewhat ironically, had been a present from Queen Victoria.

Years later, the great gun Sevastopol was dug out from its mountain grave and brought to the new capital to become a symbol of national pride and unity. Apparently, however, a weapon of shock and awe in nineteenth-century Africa does not look so formidable in the context of a modern traffic intersection. Sevastopol looked disappointingly small in the middle of the roundabout. A larger copy was quickly made, and it was this simulation of Sevastopol that was unveiled to great pomp before the public. The original was soon forgotten, and the copy gradually became more real than its handcrafted progenitor.

Only a block away from the roundabout of Sevastopol stands another important historical site, which Sosina points out as we walk past: the cinema of Menelik II. Not especially grand, as old cinemas go, but of the utmost symbolic value for Ethiopia, being the first cinema in the empire. Watching phantoms hurtle across a screen was strange enough in Paris and London, in the beginning. How much stranger must it have been in a country as isolated from the engines of modernity as Ethiopia?

Menelik, more successfully than Tewodros, was a moderniser. To explain the concept of a cinema, he built one and frequented it with the Empress. To introduce the concept of the bicycle, he imported two and the Royal couple rode them through the streets.

This vision of the royal cyclists Sosina loves. In fact Menelik is, hands-down, Sosi's favourite emperor; she loves how forward-thinking he was. She especially likes the story of the electric chair, wherein it is said that Menelik, having heard of this technological advance for enlightened human execution, ordered three for his kingdom. Unfortunately it was only when they were imported and assembled that he realised what in retrospect might have been obvious: they required an external electricity supply, something totally lacking at that time in his country. But, ever the lateral thinker, Menelik made a silk purse from an expensive foreign sow's ear by co-opting one of the chairs into service as his throne, a seat for which he needed no external power.

In establishing Addis Ababa, Menelik also solved the centuries-old Ethiopian problem of the royal capital that must keep moving because of scarce resources, by planting Australian eucalypt trees. Thousands, millions of them. He imported eucalypt seeds to plant all across the otherwise denuded site on which he wanted to base his capital. Eucalypts, it was found, grew like weeds in the local climate; they shot up at such speed that the dearth of wood for fuel and building purposes could at last be circumvented.

To this day, Addis is characterised by its eucalypts.

Sosi and I continue on and before too long find ourselves outside the Sheraton.

The Sheraton Addis is unparalleled for its services and appointments. It is the worm of Western comfort burrowed within the unwashed apple of the city. Like a worm, it has hollowed out a space for itself. Like a worm, it wriggles, glistening in the sunlight: the countless fountains of the many pools in the rose-spangled gardens. Its Muslim owner, an expatriate Ethiopian billionaire, was inspired (or someone was) by the fabulous watery gardens of the Moors in Andalucia: Seville's Alcázar and the Generalife of the Alhambra in Granada.

I hardly need to mention the high walls.

For our entrance to the Sheraton, Sosi dons the knock-off Prada sunglasses encrusted with diamantes that she bought from a two-dollar shop in Footscray. She looks every inch the movie star.

The front gate features a section of roadway that can lift up instantly to block the progress of any terrorist-driven vehicles proposing to ram through the boom gates and drive a shitload of explosives into heaven via the Sheraton lobby. Ethiopia, after many years of quasi-Communist rule and closeness to the Soviets under General Mengistu, is now more neutrally aligned. The greatest terrorist threat is most likely from Somali Islamists, against whom Ethiopia remains at war along her eastern border.

This security feature is comforting for guests and visitors alike.

The lobby (Sheratons don't allow for effete English *foyers*), tranquil and lofty with the deft ugliness of every five-star chain, features, when we visit that December, an oversized artificial Christmas tree surrounded with oversized pretend Christmas presents. This is presumably intended as a joyful touch, but the guests, crouched in heavy armchairs, nibbling salted nuts, ignore it. I am curious as to the identity of these guests of ultra-privilege, the new emperors of Addis. I suppose the answer is banal: international business types, African politicians and high-level bureaucrats. Perhaps, to spice things up, one or two undercover CIA or Mossad agents.

Out by the pool, eating pizzas in their swimwear, I spy the entire KLM crew of flight attendants from my flight a few days earlier. This must be their midweek layover, a minibus to the Sheraton from the airport and back again. Do they ever venture out beyond the parapets?

Sosi has spent a small fortune (the equivalent of US$350) on her three-month swimming pool membership.

'I need it!' she says. 'It is my only time in Addis for myself. I can come here every day, swim, get fit again after the baby.'

She picks up a fluffy white towel from the attendants' desk at the change rooms.

'And my friend here: he's my guest for today,' she tells them.

'Certainly,' the woman purrs. 'That will be eighteen dollars.'

Eighteen US dollars for a swim in a pool! Eighteen dollars is more than enough to deter any passing riffraff who, having made it past the boom gate and the lobby security checks, might feel in need of a cooling dip. Eighteen dollars would deter me, too. Next time, I would wait at the bar and have a beer while Sosi swims. But just this once I pay the money for the full pool experience.

The tropical sun bores into the tops of our heads as if concentrated through a magnifying glass. The poolside barbecue area and bar are quiet, poised for some later fashionable crowd. Everything around the pool is crisp, clean and ordered, the grass refreshingly thick and crunchy beneath my bare feet as I wander back out of the little wooden changing booth, all the concerns in the world sublimated into the search for a vacant lounge chair.

I see one by the KLM aircrew.

Where has Addis Ababa disappeared to? It's a thought that drifts across my mind, otherwise weighed down with squinting against the sun and keeping my towel tucked around my waist. I realise that a large painted scene of nondescript equatorial greenery has been erected above the fence all along the side that looks down the hill into the backblocks of the city. Dirt, goats, people crapping. I kind of do know what's behind there but I suppose the logic is that it would be unpleasant at these prices to have to look at it right now.

Reclining on a lounger on the perfect grass, shaded, the first thing I notice is that I belong here. The crisply starched staff are black, but the guests white. In this warped paradise, I am normal again.

Sosi trudges over to me, wrapped in a towel, as if stepping over every old circus injury she has ever suffered. She looks a little short and very black, in her snowy towel.

'This is weird today,' she says. 'Normally there are a few more locals. Perhaps it is the weekend – they do things with their family?'

She is not really expecting me to have the answer, to this or anything else, at the Addis Sheraton.

A white woman nearby plays on the grass with two black babies, by a parked four-wheel-drive-style stroller that may as well have optional airbags. I speculate that the woman must be an extravagantly paid nanny, imported from Switzerland on the strength of her gold-plated nanny resumé, working for some African bigwig busy on official duty in a hotel conference room or entertaining the American Ambassador. But Sosi tells me that she will be a common Western baby-adopter, who has just collected her new twins and is catching her breath in the shady wormhole of the Sheraton before the long flight home.

The last emperor of all, Haile Selasse, who ruled Ethiopia from 1916 until 1974, first as Regent and then as Emperor, has left behind many memories and memorials in Addis Ababa, despite the efforts of his military successors to erase him. Selasse was deposed following widespread unrest in the early 1970s, in a coup led by General Mengistu that led to the establishment of the Marxist–Leninist regime they called the Derg (a name that conjures its murky, violent nature). Mengistu, who would himself be ejected from power in 1991 in another coup – courtesy of the current governing party, the Ethiopian People's Revolutionary Democratic Front (EPRDF) – ignominiously dispatched the Emperor from his palace on 12 September 1974, in a Volkswagen Beetle.

One day, during my week in Addis, Amaha and Sosina take me to visit the Ethnological Museum on the campus of the Addis Ababa University. The museum, we discover, is housed in a former palace, which Haile Selasse used in the pre-war times before moving to the grander hillside estate now home to the president. The museum occupies the first floor of the building, up a sweeping staircase. It features displays of artifacts and videos of tribal rituals from some of the many language groups of Ethiopia. One particularly striking black-and-white video shows the coming of age ceremony for the young men of the Hamer tribe who, tradition has it, impress their elders and future brides by running stark naked across the backs of a line of cattle assembled side by side. Bits flapping, much excitement and adrenalin.

A lone museum guard stands at the far end of this hall, near a doorway, unmoving. As we approach, this old man asks us if we would also like to see the few rooms beyond the doorway. 'They were the private quarters of the Emperor Haile Selasse,' he tells us. 'No photographs!'

We are the only visitors. Haile Selasse's bedroom has been preserved as if he had just stepped out for morning coffee in 1930-something: it is passably imperial but at the same time austere and simple. His dressing room next door is a large square chamber walled on all sides with built-in wooden wardrobes.

Glass cabinets atop these wardrobes display some of the personal gifts the Emperor received from foreign heads of state: a vase from King George, a punchbowl from General de Gaulle, etc. The adjacent bathroom is exactly of its time and à la mode, its green tiles, deco porcelain and Italian fittings reminding me of old bathrooms you still come across sometimes in middle-class Australian homes. Only oversized.

It all puts me in mind of the Polish writer Ryszard Kapuściński's classic book *The Emperor*, in which Haile Selasse's former staff and servants re-live stories of the last days of the imperial court. When Kapuściński interviewed them, they were hiding in the backstreets of Addis Ababa from the death squads of the Derg.

Kapuściński paints an irresistible picture (irresistible in spirit, even if its veracity has since been questioned) of an absolute monarchy in the tradition of the Bourbon kings of Versailles. In the morning, it's said, the Emperor would stroll in his gardens, feeding his lions in their cages, while the three competing branches of the secret service would take it in turns to whisper their reports of the latest court intrigues, popping out from behind trees. One servant had the task for ten years of wiping the shoes of dignitaries when the Emperor's favourite lapdog pissed on them. Another functionary was in charge of the imperial foot-cushions; he needed to have at his disposal a complete set of cushions of varying sizes so that he was ready to insert, at exactly the right moment, the particular cushion perfectly proportioned to bridge the gap between the Emperor's feet and the floor, given the varying heights of the many different thrones around the country and the world upon which his diminutive royal highness needed to impose his presence.

I look at the old guard.

'Have you worked here for a long time?'

He nods. 'You know, I grew up in the palace,' he says. 'In the service of the Emperor.'

Amazing that, after so many years of military dictatorship, he has quietly managed to re-emerge and resume his place at his beloved Emperor's bedside, even if the Emperor, like Elvis, has long ago left the building.

'Do you know that book?' I ask him. 'A Polish writer, he came to interview many of Haile Selasse's servants not long after the coup, in the seventies.'

I am not quite sure if he has understood what I am talking about.

But to my great delight he leans over to me and grins: 'I am in that book you mention. You can find me. I am Mamo!'

All of this is new to Sosi, too, because how often are you a tourist in your hometown?

I wish he had allowed us to take photographs. What would have been the harm? But perhaps, somehow, the post-imperial authorities aren't even aware of the existence of these fully pre-served private chambers of the former king of kings. Perhaps their old guard and guardian manages to keep them secret here, at the back end of the university museum, where only ineffectual foreigners are likely to discover them.

After the museum we visit the remnants of the imperial lion pride, dozing in cages in a depressingly decrepit amusement garden. Sosi and I gaze at them through the bars.

'I will take you to visit the circus on Tuesday, your last day in Addis,' she says to me.

'The circus is still running, then?' Meaning: even after the debacle in Australia, the scandal that erupted around Marc LaChance, his sudden death, his ghost?

'We have worked hard to build the circus up again since those times,' says Shewalem, the director of Circus Addis Ababa, one of the offshoots of Circus Ethiopia since it was split up after Marc LaChance's death. Small and strong and fired with energy,

Shewalem is dressed in a crimson gymnast's tracksuit with loud branded stripes and a matching red cap. Sosi knew Shewalem as a young trainer with Circus Ethiopia. He has welcomed us into the circus' office, situated in the same bungalow as it was in Sosi's day, behind the patchwork corrugated-iron fence on the hillside above the city. Gold-painted trophies, goblets and coloured ribbons won in gymnastics competitions festoon his desk, the shelves behind, and the green-painted walls of the room around him. Just some of the triumphs of the circus troupe. Despite all of this, it's clear that the circus has nothing like the resources it once had. Without LaChance's contacts and entrepreneurial skills, it can no longer tour; it struggles to survive.

Shewalem agrees to pose briefly behind his desk for a photograph, then: 'Sosi!' he repeats, bounding up again. 'It is *so good* to see you! I must show you our *resources room!*'

He glides us into a modest room, with a few shelves of books and magazines. On a long trestle table, a row of three old personal computers. These computers were bought second-hand with some of the money Sosina raised in Australia when she organised a benefit night at a Circus Oz performance.

'The kids come here every day, after school,' she tells me proudly. 'When they are not training, they can learn things on the computers. They can teach themselves to type.'

It becomes clear that Sosina, understandably, is something of a hero at the new Circus Ethiopia (Addis Ababa). She, alone among all of their alumni who have gone on to bigger and better performance careers in foreign countries – Australia, Europe, North America – continues to support the circus, financially and organisationally, according to Shewalem. He shows me how, in appreciation, they have pinned a gold medal on top of a poster on a wall, so that it hangs around the neck of a young Sosina, who (in the poster) is smiling for the camera with her head between her feet, advertising a Circus Ethiopia tour to Germany back in the nineties.

'Sosi!' he proclaims, 'The only one who doesn't forget us!'

Further up the hill, in the brick rectangle that is their rehearsal hall, Shewalem shows us the dilapidated state of their rehearsal drum kit. Several of the skins have broken. It would cost US$400 to get them fixed – a small fortune in Addis Ababa. Shewalem is keen to draw the problem of the drums to our attention. This could be the next generous contribution from their greatest benefactor. Surely Sosi could raise $400 in Australia? (One benefit night could raise ten or twenty times as much.)

In the late afternoon all the children and young adults of the circus put on a performance in the concrete-floored rehearsal hall in honour of Sosina's visit. To be as hospitable as possible, they bring out popcorn and incense, and perform a coffee ceremony. We are the only audience. There is music, dancing, acrobatics, costumes. A cast of twenty-five. This would have been Sosi out there, in her day; one of these glowing energetic youths.

Three young boys perform a highly skilled cigar box–juggling act, tossing the boxes in circles in the air, snatching them away from gravity. They stand in line so that the nine boxes make a message: *Wel Come Sose And David To Circus Addis Ababa.* And after some artful flipping and general rearrangement: *Sose We Thank U Support Your School All Time.*

Afterwards the cast flops on the practice mats and Sosi gives an impromptu speech, advising them to work hard and pursue their dreams. They wrap their elbows around their knees and gaze up at her. She offers some technical advice to those staying back late for training on the web ropes, tucking her fake-Prada glasses on her head above her cap.

But what about those drums? It sounds like a good idea to me. Maybe I should pay for it myself? What does Oxfam say – $60 buys a goat? So $400 buys a drum kit for a needy children's circus. But would six and two-third goats be a better way to spend the money? If I had $400 in my pocket now, should I just hand it over? I would feel like a god, and exchange my guilt for a rich feeling of munificence.

Sosi, though, remains noncommittal.

She tells me flatly, outside: 'I am not going to pay to fix up their drum kit! They need everything, so much equipment!'

I'm confused now. 'But you did bring juggling clubs for them last time, and costumes?'

'Sure, I bring things; whatever I can,' she says. 'But what they need now is a *website*, so that they can sell their show. I will raise money to pay for a new website, and help them make one, find some local designers here in Addis. They need a website to get out into the world. They still have drums that they can use.'

I think to myself: *This is a woman who knows clearly in her own mind what is what.*

6

Mister Fun

'Melbourne smells very earthy,' remarks Sosina.

We are sitting in the Dancing Dog café in Footscray, in Melbourne's multicultural west, some months after that first trip of mine to Ethiopia. For months at a time in 2010 and 2011, we meet here at the Dancing Dog once a week for morning coffee and she tells me all her stories.

'Whereas Europe,' she continues, 'has a kind of pastry smell.'

I ponder this idea. 'What about Addis?'

She considers for a moment: 'Addis smells of frankincense. Every time I turn up in Addis at the airport, I smell that,' she says. 'It's the smell of my childhood, the incense smoke that comes with the coffee ceremony. And at holiday times, Ethiopian new year and Easter,' she says, 'the whole city seems like it is full of smoke, because everybody's baking traditional big breads at home and all the smoke comes up, the coffee and the smells, they're all mixed up. There are grasses, too, that smell beautiful; fresh grasses that they place on the floor under the coffee ceremony.'

We begin to do an inventory of the senses. The sounds of Addis: animals, people, cars, trucks – noises jostling in the air. Prayer sounds from the churches, from the mosques. The boys leaning out from the blue minibuses, calling out their destinations: *Mexico, Mexico, Mexico! Hiolet, Hiolet, Hiolet!* The shoeshine guys on the side of the road: the clicking sound they make when they tap their wooden brushes against the side of the little platform, the signal for you to change legs.

Sights, I ask: what does Addis look like in your dreams? 'When I think of it,' she says, 'I always see Addis from the railway station the French built, looking up the hill, up Churchill Road towards Piazza and the old city hall. If you walk there you can pass all the beautiful buildings from the Haile Selasse days: the commercial bank, the national theatre, the golden circle bank. That view, that's the sign for me, the Addis postcard.'

'We never went there, did we?' I say.

She says, 'Yes, we did. It was where those boys were, with the raw-meat bones they'd scavenged from a butcher, lighting a fire among the dirt and rocks.'

'I never saw that view,' I say. I never looked back up the hill to see that view. (I was looking at those boys.)

'Then, at night-time,' she continues, 'there is not much light in the city, and you see all of those beautiful girls on the street, and you think, would this happen if we were a rich country?'

In the dim backroom of the Dancing Dog, Sosi recounts to me the tale of her flight into asylum.

She first arrived in Australia in 1998 with Circus Ethiopia at the age of seventeen. It was February, and a plane trip that began in bitter Frankfurt and seemed like it would never end finally deposited the troupe in Adelaide, where it was 42 degrees in the shade. Four kids to a room in a backpackers' hostel without air-conditioning. Out the window, not a person to be seen. Shadows sharp as daggers.

These were supposedly the luckiest kids in Ethiopia. This was the first leg of a new four-month tour, beginning with their first ever visit to Australia and continuing to France and beyond. Marc LaChance's children's circus had become an international success, with tour after tour to Europe: Germany, Denmark, Holland. Western audiences had flocked to see their shows, to marvel at these talented, exuberant youngsters, black and therefore 'exotic' but always cheerful and fresh-faced: unthreatening. Circus Ethiopia was the latest in a long line of African (or quite often 'African') entertainments brought to Europe since the American Negro troupes of the twenties. These far from wealthy kids from Addis had travelled as their friends never could, learnt about distant cultures, seen firsthand what others could only watch on television.

But now they were on the cusp of adulthood and seeing their situation with new eyes. There was something very wrong inside their circus.

Here the story starts to swirl. How can I pay proper attention to all its subtleties and complications? It is one of those tales so shocking and unexpected for those involved, like Sosina, that it continues to jostle itself into shape long after it began. Even for her, as a seventeen-year-old, reality was shifting quickly and everything sped up in a crescendo those first few weeks in Australia. In the fifteen years since, she has never stopped working at the puzzle of it, piecing it together, asking questions wherever she comes across someone who was there: What did *you* know? How come you *didn't* know?

After we talked that day in the café I wrote a first version, almost entirely wrong. Or if not wrong, insufficiently attuned, simplifying, cutting corners. Leaping to conclusions.

The headline: Marc LaChance, it came to be revealed, was a paedophile. After it all began to come out, he fought then fled then finally posted a confession on the Internet and killed himself in Chile. (So this, it occurs to me for the first time, is the other suicide that cuts across our path, Sosina's and mine; a very different death.) But the chain of events that precipitated this dramatic climax and those that spilled out in its wake could fill many different volumes.

In the first version of this chapter there was one paragraph Sosi liked: 'Perhaps you should put that at the start?' she said. I had written: *This is all Sosina's story, the version she remembers and recounts for me at the Dancing Dog café. I think of Joske, whose name I have changed. I think of Marc LaChance's mother. I think of all the other kids among the twenty-nine, grown-up now, scattered through the suburbs and across the world. They would each have a version, too, of these events, flickering somewhere, which they might tell me (or might not). But this is about listening to Sosina.*

So I listen.

'You have to imagine,' she says, 'how we saw it at that time, when we were still kids. He was a nice guy. He was responsible for everything we had together. He did so much for all of us. He looked after us; he cared for us. He was like a normal guy. He didn't dress weird or anything. And we didn't know at that time there was even such a thing as *gay* in Ethiopia, let alone someone who wanted to have sex with young boys. In Australia, kids are taught: *Don't talk to strangers.* You'd never say that in Ethiopia.

'We used to hang out at his house in Addis. All the kids would go there. He had a nice house: good food, cartoons and movies, computer games, beds, a nice shower.

'He was Mister Fun. He even had a Michael Jackson mask. But, if you're thinking that sounds creepy, to us then it wasn't creepy. We didn't know what he was also doing. Nobody talked about that. That's why it was so hard to believe.

'There were little things that happened, and then when other stories came out later, in the time leading up to us coming to Australia, as we were travelling and learning more about what goes on in the world and what some people do, I began to think back to those earlier events and see them differently.

'For instance, there was one little boy I remembered who used to say things. The loud boy, I thought of him. He liked playing a game with coins on the ground outside at the circus. We told him to stop because gambling was a bad thing. This annoyed him, so he would say, loudly: *If you trouble me, I'm going to come out and say something about that guy. You know who,* he would say, to scare us. *What are you going to say?* we'd ask him. And one day he said: Bushti! *He's a* bushti! *He likes ass.* The little boy was seven years old so all the other kids took no notice. They told him to shut up. He was a Felasha, an Ethiopian Jew; he left soon afterwards for Israel along with all the other Felasha.'

'And one time,' Sosi says, 'I asked Marc LaChance: *Why don't you have a wife?* We were at his house. I was just curious, because in my experience anyone of his age would have a wife. He laughed and said he used to have a girlfriend. He showed me some pictures of a young girl in Canada on a horse. It looked like it was from a while ago.

'*But why don't you have a wife now?* I asked him.

'*Well, you know,* he said, pointing to his wooden floor, which had little indentations all across it, *my girlfriend came here with her high heels; she was dancing around the house. Look at the little dots,* he said. *From her heels dancing around, you know; look at the mess she made!*

'And he laughed. At the time I believed him; only when I looked back did I think, *Oh, he was joking!*'

She remembers: Marc LaChance had a tea farm and a holiday house in Sri Lanka. He used to go there once a year for four weeks. All the photos he brought back were of young boys.

Another night, Sosi and a boyfriend dropped in to visit Marc at his house. He was by himself watching a film. Sosi and her friend asked: 'Can we watch?' He looked at them. They were older by now; sixteen or so. He said, 'You'll be fine, sit down.' The movie was in French, and it turned out to be about a boy with sexual problems. At one point the boy in the movie took a piece of meat out of a fridge, cut it open and had sex with it. Sosi couldn't believe what they were looking at and that the director of their children's circus was showing it to them.

'I spoke a long time later,' Sosi says, 'with someone who used to know Marc in those days. He said Marc had sexual problems. He couldn't get excited sexually in normal circumstances; he could only get excited when he didn't want to. It reminded me of that boy in the film, opening the fridge…'

For the boys who suffered most from Marc LaChance, she says, people assume it must have been about money or manipulation; but it all comes down to the most basic thing – trust. It all comes down to being cared for, looking out for someone to care for you and love you. Some of the kids came from an orphanage, some came from the streets—

It's not necessary to tell everything. Parts of the story of Marc LaChance we have written in and written out again, because Sosi wants to make sure people he has damaged are not damaged further by our storytelling. What matters more, what I long for, even though it is perhaps impossible, is to understand exactly how it was and what it means *only from* Sosina's point of view, and then to have you understand it, too. I want you not to think light brown is dark brown. I want you not to jump where you might tiptoe. I want you to share the glorious surprise of seeing things from another side.

I'm not sure if any of this makes sense. Where I'm writing now, Sosina is far away, across the southeast corner of Australia (see, even now I want you not to misinterpret me: our continent is such that a corner can be large). A westerly wind is blowing the fear of fire into these mountains. Tomorrow will be a scorcher. Marc LaChance is dead. Or not: Sosi sometimes wonders. He might have slipped into another skin in South America; he wouldn't be the first.

There are always things I'm not telling. And who knows what Sosi's not telling me? It's hard to imagine how the not-telling must work in the mind of a paedophile. How the double life is negotiated, the betrayals massaged. The siren call of flesh, and the mind that can step across into the dark margins of the possible. Outside here, the cicadas pulse, as they have all day and will tomorrow. The pulse that quickens in his veins as he lifts the sleeping child from the couch and carries him to his bed. And the pulse in the not-sleeping child who pretends to sleepwalk back to the safety of the couch, the strongest silent grinding of resistance.

Sosina has been forensic in her research. LaChance had European circus friends: trainers, directors. Sosi keeps in touch with those she can, and she has asked each of them the question (sometimes in person, sometimes on Facebook): *How come you didn't know? You were from the West. Now that I've lived in the West I can recognise different sexual desires. How come you didn't realise then what Mark LaChance was like?* And each of them has told her: *I knew that he was gay, sure, but I didn't pick up that he loved young boys. That's another thing altogether.*

A truth that cuts sharp against the grain will always be elusive. We can only see what we have already seen.

Oh, and one other thing I might misinterpret, or you might, or we might be wondering. Sosina says: 'By the time we left for Australia, some of the Ethiopian circus trainers in Addis had their suspicions. It was not as if they did nothing, and they certainly weren't stupid. They tried to handle it without the whole thing exploding, the circus collapsing.' (The whole world, from her perspective.) They wanted to give him the benefit of the doubt because he was the founder. Later, she found out that they had confronted him: they'd warned him quietly that he would have to leave the circus and the country if he didn't stop. Apparently he cried and cried.

Friends of Marc LaChance would come to visit the circus in Addis Ababa. Sometimes they brought boys with them. Nobody could fail to notice the expensive clothes they wore. One of the men was David Christie. Christie ran an orphanage at Jari in Ethiopia's south Wollo region for a Swiss NGO, Terre des Hommes. One time Marc LaChance took the circus down to Jari to perform for the local children. The aim was to inspire them to start their own circus, which they did. LaChance also recommended a Canadian friend of his to Christie as an English teacher. But this paedophile, Denys Benjamin, was insufficiently discreet. After only a few weeks Christie had to sack him when employees complained he had taken a 12-year-old boy to bed. Christie himself was finally caught in the act at the end of 1996 during a Christmas party for the children. His lengthy absence from the party, which was not entirely unprecedented, aroused suspicion. Staff discovered a half-naked boy climbing out Christie's bedroom window. Terre des Hommes fired Christie but chose not to inform the Ethiopian authorities (a decision the charity afterwards regretted), instead allowing Christie to leave the country and settle quietly in a London suburb. The story only came out publicly after a *Guardian* newspaper investigation, prompted in turn by an Australian newspaper report that a group of Ethiopian circus children touring Australia had accused their circus' director of being a paedophile but had been refused asylum.

But we're getting ahead of ourselves. One thing leads inexorably to another.

The business about Marc LaChance, the gradual disintegration of his masquerade, as if his sunny face had been dipped into a slow-acting acid bath, shimmered in the deathly silences of Adelaide. I remember seeing Circus Ethiopia at the Adelaide Festival, although of course I didn't know Sosina then. They played the great old barn of His Majesty's Theatre. The mood emanating from that stage I interpreted as unalloyed youthful joy. I'm sure that wasn't faked: when a performer steps on stage she can leave behind her daily cares, as can the audience in the stalls who, for the price of entry, have been invited in to share a gift. But in the corridors and the green room, well beyond any vague and rosy feelings of solidarity I was holding on to as I mooched off to the next show, there were currents shifting.

Sosina tells me: 'We could have been anywhere. We never had dreams of living in Australia. What did we know about Australia?' (She knew it only from her schoolroom maps: *The first place that will sink.*) 'It was just the first stop of the tour and everything fell apart so quickly.'

It wasn't only Marc LaChance's wandering hands and thoughts, his infinite ability to lie or be blind or not care or be unable to resist or all of these that were the problem – although these were problem enough. The problem was also that, at any moment, he could have been exposed back in Addis, and the whole world opened by the circus could have disappeared as if it had never been. There was no solidity to its existence. For years the young performers had been promised that the circus was raising money to establish a proper home base in Addis, a place to train and develop sustainable careers. They wouldn't be children forever. Some were young adults already. Sosi and her friends were only too aware of this, even if it has become increasingly evident in retrospect that children were all that interested LaChance and his friends. At every performance on their European trips the performers had raised money for the home base. Their token wage rate of 5 German Marks or AU$10 per week was always justified like this: the remainder of the money the circus earns will go towards the home base. The home base! Where was any sign that the home base was materialising? Where was any sign of all that money?

As a child, you don't question. You are the luckiest kids in Ethiopia. You travel the world. But what will happen afterwards? When all you've wanted since you were six years old, like the cigarette seller teaching herself contortion on the lounge room floor, is to make a career like this, performing circus: what choices would remain in Addis if Marc LaChance destroyed it all?

Sosi talked to other artists from around the world at the Adelaide Festival club. It came up in conversation: *How much do you get paid? We're supposed to get $10 a week, although actually they haven't paid us anything here yet. There's some problem with the money. …$10 a week!?? Are you serious?* In their faces she could see just how far this was from normal in their world.

The Australian newspaper *The Age* later reported that the income from the circus' Australian tour was thought to be about $90,000 but that none of the performers was being paid.

As the tour rolled on from Adelaide to Canberra and finally to Sydney, where at last the streets were populated and the city breathed and laughed, unhappiness rippled through the circus.

'You could sense that there was something in the air, something big was coming up,' Sosina says, 'but you weren't sure what.' Nobody knew whom he or she could trust to talk to, so most things went unsaid. Their parents were far away and couldn't help them; anyway, their parents still believed Marc LaChance had brought only miracles and kindness with his circus.

At a meeting one day there was a sudden breaking point. Sosina watched as some of her friends began speaking out, as if they no longer cared for the consequences. One after another they stood up and spoke their minds: *You're not paying us! You said that you were raising money for the home base! We want to know where the money is! When are you going to start looking after the kids who've worked so long for this circus?* They didn't have to mention Marc LaChance explicitly.

Sosi was trying to work out what was going on. She asked her close friend, Sabla, after the meeting: 'Why did you say that? Don't you know that when you go back to Ethiopia they're not going to put you in the circus any more? Aren't you afraid of that?'

Sabla said: 'I don't care.' And the next day she was gone.

7

Asylum

In Sydney, *Titanic* was playing at the cinemas on George Street. It was close by where the circus troupe was staying, at the YMCA in Surry Hills; an easy outing. The troupe were taken to it three times; they had to go everywhere together. The third occasion was at the very end of the tour. After their last performance, they had a few free days in Sydney before the flight out for the next leg of the tour in Europe.

They were all gathered outside the cinema on the pavement, about to go in, when one of the elders in the group, in his early twenties, pointed to their feet. 'You, you and you,' he said, 'You don't have proper shoes! You can't go in like that. You need to go back to the hostel and get some covered shoes.' He said to the tour manager, 'I will take them back to get some proper shoes and we will meet you in the theatre.' He took them; there were eight, plus him made nine. The others watched them walk away along the footpath, then went into the cinema.

Mel, who was a good friend of Sosi's at that time, said to her: 'This is it.'

'What do you mean, *this is it?*'

'They're not coming back,' he said.

'What do you mean, *they're not coming back?*'

'I'm telling you,' said Mel, 'they're not coming back.'

Sosi and Mel went into the cinema with the rest and sat down to watch *Titanic*.

Sosi tells me how she cried and cried and cried in that movie, not because the movie was so sad but because of what Mel had said and the feeling that it was their beautiful, fragile circus inexorably sinking.

Sure enough, the nine who had left for proper shoes never turned up at the cinema. The movie ended and the rest of the troupe went back to the hostel. They knocked on doors and looked in rooms.

The nine had vanished.

Eight boys and young men, one girl. Some of them had left their clothes behind in their rooms. Sosi remembers sitting in her own room, thinking: *This is the end of it. If those kids go and any secrets come out publicly about the circus or Marc LaChance that will be the end of my life as well; the end of my career.* She saw her life folding in upon itself, smaller and smaller. In other rooms other kids sat, with their own thoughts.

The tour manager called them all together for a meeting. He tried to comfort them. 'Don't worry,' he said, 'I'm sure they're still around. And if they have run away they'll be caught and brought back. We'll always have the circus. We're on our way to Europe, more shows!'

'But everyone,' Sosi tells me, 'everyone was in their own brain, thinking. Worrying.'

Mel talked to her; he tried to talk to everyone. He was close to many of the girls in the troupe, because they could speak to him about things that troubled them. The girls asked him, 'What do you want to do?'

He replied 'What do *you* want to do?' He wanted to find out what they were thinking – was anyone else planning to leave? He couldn't ask straight out, only go around the question sideways.

The next night in the hostel, the circus kids were watching television. There on the news already they saw their friends, the ones who had fled. They had somehow got themselves to Melbourne and onto the news. They had announced that they were seeking asylum, due to the ongoing regime of abuse they had faced in the circus over a number of years which, as *The Age* would put it, 'the Ethiopian Government had been unable to prevent'. They were refusing to go back.

Later the same evening, Sosi visited her friend Abey in his room. She found him at the basin, washing his shorts. She watched him washing his shorts for ages, standing at the basin, lost in thought. She went away and came back and he was still there, washing his shorts. She said to him, 'Abey, what's going on?'

He said, 'Nothing,' but she said, 'Abey, you've been washing your shorts for ages.' She left him there. In the morning Abey and a friend of his did not appear for breakfast. Their rooms were empty. A little later, it was discovered that two other boys had left separately, so now thirteen were gone in all.

This was on the second-last day before the flight.

Mel and Sosi talked again. They saw that their time was running out. The circus was collapsing. If they went on with the tour it might be their last. If they ran away to join the others – they had no idea what future they would face. But now they knew their rights. If they left and somebody stopped them, they could refuse to leave. They could seek asylum.

Sosi was upset about the kids who were left behind, the girls that she had known since she was eight years old. When she spoke to them and asked them how they were feeling, they said they were scared. She could see they weren't brave enough to run away in this strange country.

The same day that Abey and the other three disappeared, Sosi and Mel took themselves downstairs. They told the others they were going for a walk. Next door to the YMCA was a hotel. Sosi and Mel went inside the hotel and booked themselves a twin-share room. Then they returned to the YMCA. That night, which was to be the last for the circus in Australia, they packed up their belongings and slipped out into the street. Meeting no one on the way, they checked into the hotel.

The next morning, by the time it was discovered that they were gone, they could be expected to be far away, hidden elsewhere in the city. Nobody would suspect they were next door.

Sosi and Mel watched out of their hotel-room window as the coach arrived to take what was left of the circus to the airport. The friends with whom they had shared ten years filed up the steps of the coach and disappeared behind the mirrored glass. Their only goodbyes were silent, distant, unobserved.

Thereafter, the circus flew off to Europe, hurriedly bringing a new bunch of performers and technicians from Addis to replace those who had stayed behind in Australia, and trying to pretend it could carry on as if none of this had happened.

The poignancy of the moment in the Sydney street, where Sosi and Mel looked down upon their frightened friends exiting their lives, seeps into the air of the Dancing Dog café, into the fabric of its creaking retro lounge chairs.

'How did you pay for the hotel room?'

'That is a good question,' she says, and grins. 'I was good at business, even in the circus! I know how to make money;

remember, I used to sell cigarettes outside the St George brewery. When I was fifteen or sixteen, we first went on tour to Europe, and I thought, *The circus has no money; they can't or won't give me any money, so I will have to make my own.*'

She had taken a collection of Ethiopian craft objects – small silver crosses, jewellery, painted wood – in her suitcase to Germany, and sold them there to local expatriate Ethiopians who came to see the show. She used to stand next to the tour manager, Gizaw, while he sold T-shirts in the foyer after every performance. One day she had a better idea. She was looking at the poster Gizaw put up in the foyer. It was a picture of a dreadlocked Ethiopian boy with beautiful teeth, smiling. It made her think of the *mefakia*, the traditional wooden stick toothbrushes sold everywhere on the streets of Addis. She rang her mum at home and asked her to send over a box of 250 *mefakia*, DHL, and she asked Gizaw to write a sign in German underneath the poster, saying: *If you want your teeth to look this good you have to buy this toothbrush.* They sold out. Sosi rang her mum to order another box for delivery to Berlin. She could sell each toothbrush to the Germans for 5 marks, but in Addis the whole box of 250 would cost that much. The other kids watched how much money she was making in the foyer after every show and, next time, they brought their own stuff to sell, too.

Sosi spent every pfennig she made in Germany on goods to take back to Ethiopia. Some of these were speculative purchases, such as the Spice Girls–style platform shoes unobtainable in Addis (before the days of cheap Chinese rip-offs) that she knew rich girls would pay a handsome price for. Some were presents for herself: her favourite of the Spice Girls' platforms. The bulk were presents for her family. All in all she managed to transport 150 kilograms worth that time, since the circus had some extra kilograms in its allowance. She took clothes, frying pans, whatever her mother needed.

After selling her collection of boots and other temptations back home in Addis, Sosi had 18,000 Ethiopian burr in her pocket, on top of all the new things at her mother's house. Such a profit from selling toothbrushes! Now that the Australian tour was approaching, she invested her surplus in small but precious items that she could sell in Australia. She made up her mind to concentrate on Ethiopian gold: rings, small crosses. When she met Ethiopian people in Adelaide, Canberra or Sydney, she would ask them if they were interested in buying gold, and in this way sold every piece that she had brought. The girl is nothing if not resourceful.

Which is how, standing with Mel at the hotel-room window, weeping as the friends she might never see again were driven off in the opaque bus to the departure lounge, Sosi at least retained the comfort of $1000 cash in her pocket.

She knew that she could pay for the hotel room. How much further the money would go, and would need to go, she had no idea. She and Mel shared a cup of hot chips for dinner, just in case.

They rang their parents. Sosi told her mother that she had decided to stay in Australia, that she wasn't coming home. Ayanalem pleaded, cried. She couldn't understand. Sosi couldn't begin to explain the reasons to her, the dark truth about Marc LaChance – wasn't he that lovely man who had come to her mother's house for dinner? The idea of different sexualities, benign or otherwise, didn't exist in Ethiopia, so far as Sosi knew. When the circus had travelled to Copenhagen she had seen a marriage on the steps of the city hall. She had watched the wedding party throwing rice, and two guys come out together wearing suits. She had waited for the bride to appear, but then the two guys had turned towards each other and started kissing and she had realised that no bride was going to appear; that this marriage was proceeding very happily with two grooms marrying each other. Sosi had snapped a photo and sent it to her mother, who responded that it wasn't real and it was evil all at the same time. Ayanalem was a highly intelligent woman, but her world was so much smaller than her daughter's, even when Sosina was not yet eighteen.

As for Tewabé, it's said he cried for two years after he heard Sosina wasn't coming home. The three of them knew that Ayanalem and Tewabé could never afford to visit Sosina in Australia, and that Sosina would not be able to travel freely to Ethiopia unless one day she won Australian citizenship. She could give them no reassurance as to her future, and they were powerless to protect her. She hung up, promising to call again – from somewhere – when she could.

On the evening news that night, Sosi and Mel saw that the four boys had also gone to Melbourne, to meet up with the first nine from the circus. Ethiopian–Australian people whom the circus troupe had met in Sydney at a barbeque had told them that the community was strongest and largest in Melbourne, so this destination was no surprise. Sosi and Mel walked across to Central Station and bought themselves tickets on the overnight train south.

The train shuffled into the darkness. Australian trains, even then, slunk around the margins of society. Airports were becoming popular shopping malls, replete with spangled donuts and huge plastic coffees. The night train was on its last legs, bewilderingly slow, smelling of failure. Only those too scared to fly or too poor for the back of the plane – those handful wanting to get off at some obscure wayside station, struck by some misplaced nostalgia for the tug and clatter of the railways or needing for some reason, like Sosi and her friend, to escape into the long anonymity of the night – scattered themselves along the windows of the carriages and pressed their breath into the glass.

For Sosi, the train led away from family, culture and memory and into the void.

In the morning, at Spencer Street Station, in the chill air of the autumn, they walked out to find an Ethiopian taxi driver who could take them to the community. They didn't have to look far.

A few days after the recounting of this story I called Sosina on the phone. It was early April, 2011. I had heard she might be travelling back to Ethiopia for a couple of months. Some kind of job that would take her there, and she could stay on and spend time with her family. It would be a great opportunity for me to meet her there again in late May and do the things we needed to do to finish off the book. We might even go to Cairo, where her brother lived his last six years, waiting to be resettled as a refugee.

'Hi, Dave,' she said, 'I've been meaning to call you. You heard about my—'

'Yes, going to Ethiopia!'

'But something has come up now: my father's sick. He has a cancer. He got a new test back yesterday. He needs to take it out but the doctor says they can't perform the operation in Ethiopia. He doesn't want to travel; he is worried something will happen to my mum. I have to sort it out. I am getting them to send over all his medical reports so that I can take them to a doctor here and see what's best, you know, and how much it would cost to treat him here. I'll try to get pro bono; if I have pro bono it will be easier to get a visa because they'll not be so worried he will try to stay on in the country.'

I couldn't stop myself from thinking, *Oh no, this is going to jeopardise the trip we might have had.* For the book. I was going to fit it in at the end of my semester in late May, straight after teaching finished. I knew this to be staggeringly petty and selfish of me, but from my point of view the book was the important thing. I had committed myself to write it; I wanted to get on and do it. I wanted to shape and craft this story, and divine the message it held for me. I found myself, despite my better instincts, impatient to box up Sosi's life and have it finished. I said to Sosi—I can't remember what I said to Sosi; I remember trying to find some words appropriate. 'My brother might be able to help,' I said. 'He works at the Children's Hospital. He knows lots of specialists.'

Maybe if everything could happen quickly, I negotiated in my own mind, she could bring her dad out soon to have the operation. He could recover and she could take him back with her when she travelled to Ethiopia. She could stay on, as she planned, and I could join her near the end of her stay. The best of all worlds.

'Only thing is, Dave,' she said, 'I have to be back in Melbourne by early June. I have a gig. I'm doing *The Burlesque Hour.*' *The Burlesque Hour* was an avant-garde theatre show with lots of nakedness and irony. Sosi wasn't planning to mention this to her parents; they wouldn't understand.

I was going to have to let things unfold as they were wont to. Besides, what did I know about caring for a father?

Sosi grew up fathered; I have been auditioning fathers all my life. Even women may apply. So long as they present wisdom and authority, are gentle, not too bullying. I love nothing better than to be instructed what to do. *Here is the problem*, I say; *Well, here is the path forward*, they reply. I am so good at following paths; I reward all my potential fathers by how well I catch on and charge off down the track, cheerful, self-sufficient, *I'll see you next time!* They must be proud of me.

My mother has never instructed me. Sometimes I wished she would. She has left space for all the fathers, from the very first, the biological one, the *real* one who was the very least real of all. I was the youngest and she said I could make up my own mind about things. She never pressured me, thank God, to do medicine or law or anything that children with good grades are told they should. She used to bring me a cup of tea in bed in the mornings before high school and I always felt that in itself was an incredible treat. A pure gift. She allowed me space to find myself and it wasn't her fault that I never did, or not for a long time.

Meanwhile, as I was fretting on news of Sosi's travel plans, on the radio there was a passing commotion. The Australian Opposition spokesman on Immigration, Scott Morrison, had questioned the use of taxpayers' money to fly a handful of asylum seekers from Christmas Island to Sydney for the funerals of their parents and siblings and children, those who drowned when their flimsy boat fell apart metres from the shore they had travelled a thousand kilometres to reach. The Opposition Leader, Mr Abbott had supported his spokesman. He, too, (the quintessential patriarch) thought *it's a trifle strange* for these people to be granted such a privilege. A week earlier Abbott had proposed cutting foreign aid to Africa, or failing that to Indonesian schools, to pay instead to rebuild roads and railways damaged by the floods in Queensland. 'I believe charity,' he said, 'begins at home.'

This is a theme nurtured on right-wing blogs and email lists and talk shows. The Opposition Leader (two years afterwards, prime minister) thinks he's on a winner with this line. *Charity begins at home.* It's not that we are not a compassionate people, we tell ourselves; on the contrary, look at the television images of us in the streets of Brisbane mopping up with our mates after their devastating tragedy.

But the funerals of those who drowned off Christmas Island were also shown on television. The media reported mutterings and misgivings expressed by *moderates* within the Opposition Leader's party.

The Opposition Leader came out and said, 'We may have crossed a line.' His spokesman for Immigration said, 'I stand by my comments but I accept that it may have been the wrong day to say them on.'

It was an understandable mistake. Usually pushing the fear-of-'illegal'-boat-people button works just fine in Australia.

But let's go back: Sosina and Mel have arrived in Melbourne for the first time, on the train.

The Ethiopian taxi driver knows exactly where to take them. The story of the asylum-seeking children and young adults is big news in the local community. At the house of a man we have decided, Sosi and I, to call Abebe, they find the other thirteen who had already left the circus. Sosi counts them up. Everyone is there. The nine who jumped ship during *Titanic* and the four boys who followed in the night. When the four arrived, a day or so later, the nine who had arrived first were suspicious. They thought the four had been sent by the company, the circus, to spy on them and coax them back into the fold. They couldn't trust anything they said until they had talked and eaten and slept and talked some more. Then they were tight. When Sosi and Mel arrived, the nine who had become thirteen were even more suspicious. Mel was a sound technician in the circus; quasi-management. The thirteen thought that Sosi and Mel had been sent by the company to spy on them and coax them back into the fold. They couldn't trust anything they said until they had talked and eaten and slept and talked some more. Then all fifteen were tight.

They all slept on Abebe's lounge room floor. Sosi says there was a mattress. There can't have been fifteen. I imagine them piled up, higgledy-piggledy, a long way from home, waking up to a strange continent and bumping each other in the ribs.

Abebe's wife cooked and cooked and cooked. Comfortingly familiar *injera* and homemade *wats*, in the vast quantities acrobats and teenagers require.

Abebe asked: 'Are you all sure you want to stay here? It's not easy; you left your family, your country, everything. Are you sure you want to live here? If you're not sure I'm going to return you to the circus. You have to be sure.'

All of the fifteen said nothing. A couple of the younger ones started crying.

'That was good he said that,' says Sosi. 'I thought he was a good leader.'

When I think of Abebe, whom I haven't met, I picture Sosi's father, Tewabé. Tall, thin, erect, a stern demeanour that cracks into a grin. The good father addressing his people. (His wife cooking and cooking and cooking all the while.)

None of the fifteen decided to go back.

It would have been cosy at first, crammed altogether in the lounge room like a litter, at night huddled on a raft of dreams floating above Addis Ababa. But it was obviously a transitional arrangement. Other Ethiopians began to drop by, helping out, picking up the kids to take them here and there.

The local Anglican church found the fifteen a house to stay in temporarily. A big house in Somerville Road, Yarraville – a suburb next to Footscray. They could move in straightaway. Outside the kitchen window was a trampoline.

For the fifteen asylum seekers, it was time to go to the Immigration Department.

The first question was: 'What's your name?'

'Sosina.'

'What's your surname?'

Pause.

'What's a surname?'

'What's your family name?'

'What's a family name?'

They don't have family names in Ethiopia, Sosi tells me. A person has her own name and her father's name. She also has her father's father's name: Sosina – Tewabé – Wogayehu.

'But if you want to live in Australia you have to have a surname.' On the spot she had to decide on one. Sosi and her interpreter agreed that the nearest thing to a surname she possessed was probably Wogayehu, the name of the grandfather she had never met.

I find this name business fascinating; the idea that you might feel you have to make up one of the most basic elements of your identity to be accepted as a potential citizen of a foreign country, as part of the process of convincing the bureaucrats of that country that you are trustworthy. I make Sosi explain it all in great detail. 'What would you write in Ethiopia if you had to sign a form?'

'Sosina Tewabé.' Her dad's name. And her dad would sign: Tewabé Wogayehu. His dad's name.

'So why didn't you tell them your name was Sosina Tewabé?'

'Because that's my dad's name. It's not my family name.'

Her dad said, when she told him about it: 'But you never met your grandfather. How come you are called by this name?'

She said to him: 'It's a long story.'

I can also imagine the scene from the point of view of the Immigration Department official. I have a bunch of African kids come in, looking very nervous, led by a few African adults. I take one at a time. I ascertain the correct form and start to fill it in. At the very first, most simple question, in which all we want to know is *Who are you?* – by which we also mean *Who are you, really?* – you don't seem to be able to give a simple answer. You look sideways and nervous and whisper with the adult helping you, as if you have a number of identities to choose from even at your young age, and you are discussing in some African language which one of those identities to front up with on this occasion.

Each of the fifteen was taken into a small room, to be inter-viewed on their own. Sosi's small room was very plain. She sat at a plain table opposite an official with a small tape recorder, and alongside an interpreter.

Again, I am the Immigration Department official. It is my job to be rigorous. It is my job to separate the worthy from the unworthy. We have only so much compassion we can spare in Australia (apparently) and, whatever my personal views or sym-pathies might be, I am charged with the job of determining who, of all those that traipse through the door into our air-conditioned offices, deserves some. Nobody likes a cheat or a freeloader.

I (the Immigration Department official) say to Sosi: 'This situation you say you have to escape from, this circus in your country, it sounds amazing. It's opened up a lot of doors for you. And this Marc LaChance, who came all the way from Canada to live in Ethiopia and run your circus. I'm sure he cares about you; I'm sure he's worried about you, here so far away from your families. Any allegations you make against the circus or your country or Marc LaChance will be very serious...' (This is how Sosi remembers the tenor of the conversation with the official. I suppose in the end it makes no difference how I imagine myself, in the role of the official: whether I am a racist who looks down on Africans, a stickler who fancies myself as a TV-barrister or cop-show detective, a tired liberal wearing myself out trying to humanise the pointy end of the system or, as is most likely, some more subtle mixture of all of these and more. The point is the policy I am enacting, an impassive wall of forms and procedures. I, whomever I might be, have the job to stamp them, sign them, clock off.)

Australia is an original signatory to the 1951 United Nations Convention relating to the Status of Refugees. The Convention was put in place to support those forced to flee their country in Europe during and after Word War II who had a *well-founded fear of being persecuted for reasons of race, religion, nationality, membership of a particular social group or political opinion* should they return. It specifies only those five grounds for asylum. It makes no mention of the rights of children or of persecution by sexual predators and paedophiles; the Convention's drafters could hardly have anticipated a situation like that faced by a group of young circus performers from Ethiopia fifty years later. This made the position of the latter that much more difficult. Even if their stories of abuse and exploitation were believed by the Immigration officials, they didn't fit into an accepted category for asylum.

Each of the fifteen had a slightly different personal experience of life in the circus under Marc LaChance, a different story to tell, a different case to make. For Sosi, she wasn't claiming to have been directly sexually abused. But she had been under the duty of care of a man who abused others and who had betrayed her trust; who might well place her in danger. She was not being paid for her work. The hopes she had nurtured all her life for a career as a performer were being dashed. If she returned home she feared what might happen next. Marc LaChance was still in control of the circus. And even if he could be exposed and arrested, if people would trust the police and legal system and come forward in Ethiopia – what then? The circus life she had worked so hard to make, trained a dozen years for, would be destroyed. Her world would shrink back to the streets of Addis. Now that she had glimpsed what she could achieve, she had so many ideas and dreams she needed to fulfil. She had only just begun and now this man, who she had trusted with her life, was killing everything.

Would Australia find reason enough in her case to accept her? Like the other fourteen, all she could do was submit an individual application for asylum to the Australian Immigration Department, sign the documents and wait.

As we read over this chapter together, Sosi says, quietly, 'You know I think about the people coming in the boats now. They're taking so much risk for themselves and their kids; they must be so desperate to put themselves on those boats.'

'I took a risk,' says Sosi, 'Everything I valued I left behind when we fled: my family, the circus, the culture I grew up with. But these people even more; they left their country, their family, their career, plus they're on the boat for they don't know how many days and can't know whether they will survive it. And they have kids with them, most of them. I think about it often: how desperate they must be to take that decision. Now that I'm a mother I think about that. Even when I fly on a plane I think about it differently, having kids. I think about travelling from A to B with my kids; will I get there safely? Even if they hope, these people, *Oh wow, my future is bright*, because probably they already know a lot about Australia, they also know how many people are dead on those waters.'

Sosina's situation was very different from that of the waves of people who have attempted to seek asylum in Australia since the post-war Jews, crossing the ocean by boat. But then, as soon as I write 'waves of people' I know I am mooshing together thousands upon thousands of individual stories, none of which I know. All of these people have families I haven't met, haven't sat down and had coffee with, in Afghanistan, Burma, Sri Lanka or wherever. Some of them might well be crooks; I bet none of them are saints. But, after all, the proud Anglo-Celtic mainstream of Australian culture is founded on a gene pool deemed criminal by the British Crown. I have an abiding fantasy that if ordinary conservative Australians – or Europeans or Americans, for that matter – could meet individual asylum seekers, share a meal and hear their stories, a lot of misconceptions would be dispelled. No matter how modern we think we are, we are still fearful of those who come from different 'tribes'. We need to rediscover rituals for meeting strangers; establish traditions like those of Indigenous communities. (There are organisations already that try to do these things.) But it's obvious that there are political interests in encouraging precisely the opposite, because fear is a powerful currency.

Sosina doesn't fit a liberal mold for a 'poor asylum seeker', a tragic victim 'we' have saved. She has fearlessness, chutzpah. Some will wonder whether she wasn't what is called, disparagingly, an 'economic migrant'. Did she *herself* have a *well-founded fear of being persecuted* as a result of being under the care of a leading member of an international paedophile ring? Why isn't her story simpler, her tragedy starker? It's as if any of us only has so much generosity, so much empathy, to spare.

The upper classes in Victorian England had a notion of the 'deserving poor' – those pitiable but virtuous souls down on their luck, *deserving* of sympathy and charity. Undeserving were those who somehow brought misfortune on themselves, through their vices. I think many of us still apply these categories today, without necessarily thinking of them, and without recognising that, almost always, it is only through the luck of our birth that we get to be the ones who make these distinctions. Who is deserving? Who gets to say? And how often do I say to myself, Australian passport in my pocket: *How lucky am I?*

8

A leap of faith

Sosina goes to the supermarket in the evening. Her baby sleeps.
All she can think about now is how to save her father. She knows
how Immigration works: there is a special short-term visa for
medical treatment. She needs that form filled in. She needs a
surgeon's signature, a hospital's approval. I have asked my brother
John. He has put out feelers to colleagues at the hospital, who
write to *their* colleagues, benignly: *The patient is a friend of a friend
of a friend…*I imagine what it must feel like to be Tewabé, Sosi's
father, in Addis Ababa, knowing that his daughter across the
ocean is the only person who might have the power to keep him
alive. Sosina says when you grow up in Ethiopia all you want to
do is help your parents. Maybe it's different in Australia? She told
an Australian friend that it might cost between twenty and forty
grand to bring her father out and have him treated. Her friend
asked: 'How old is he?'

'Seventy or so,' she said.

And her friend said: 'Wow, that's a big investment! Is it worth it?'

She will find the money somehow, if and when it comes to that. She's not so concerned about the money at the moment. The first thing is the form and the signatures.

We hear back from John's networks. One doctor warns that, even if a surgeon agrees to take the patient on, the problem will be the hospital bureaucracy. He has been involved in a case like this before. They waited a long time for approvals and in the meantime the patient died. The hospitals are already overcrowded. There is a competing queue of deserving local cases. A man in Ethiopia dying of cancer: this is of course very sad. But: *a friend of a friend of a friend*. Where does that leave you? We know full well how many other equally sad stories will be out there, especially in the *Third World*. This doctor suggests Bangkok might be a better option. Treatment is cheaper there, they have good doctors and facilities; they are set up for *medical tourism*. There is a direct flight to Bangkok from Addis. This is all very logical, and generous of the man to even spend the time replying to the email. But—

Sosina wants to bring her father to her hometown for treatment, where she can take care of him. He can recover at her house, eat her food, sleep on her pillows, be entertained by his granddaughter. Glimpse her new life. She could never coax him earlier to visit, when he was well. She would have paid for his ticket back then, but he wouldn't leave Ayanalem who, tied to her oxygen tanks, with her weak lungs and weak heart, was already too ill to fly.

Another doctor replies. His email is more encouraging. Sosi will follow up with this one.

'You know,' she reflects, one day when we are talking at the Dancing Dog, 'I would have given up by now if not for Mel. He tells me: *Look at everything you have done so far in your life to get to this point; this is just another thing that you can do.*'

And I think to myself, this is one thing we share, Sosi and I: the strength afforded by our spouses. Oftentimes when I have been anxious about whatever it might be, Linda has talked me down. We are, both of us, lucky on that count.

Sosina and Mel now have a mortgage. Sosi used the money she saved working at Circus Oz to pay for the deposit on a brick-and-tile-roofed house in a quiet street in a suburb called St Albans. St Albans is not a fashionable suburb, which means it is affordable, but it is sure to skyrocket in value over the next few years. With the baby still little, Mel is earning most of the money at his flash new job in IT with a big firm.

Their house is on one of those huge flat blocks that used to be normal in the Australian suburbs. It doesn't even look particularly large, with the brick house plonked roughly in the middle of the rectangle and wide shaggy lawns stretching front and back. It is probably bigger in square metres than Sosi's parents' compound back in Addis. One day, Sosi and Mel might pursue the Aussie dream and renovate. Put a deck on. That sort of thing. They already have a massive old brick garage and shed that could be converted into a granny flat.

St Albans is on a train line to the north-west of Melbourne. I can't quite picture how far north and how far west it is, which disconcerts me because I like to know where places are. I like to be able to visualise them on a map. The second time I visited Sosi in St Albans I thought it would be a pleasant adventure to ride my bike there. I knew she lived quite close to the Maribyrnong River, and I knew there was a bike path that followed that river upstream. If I rode along one of the straight roads due west from my place, in Brunswick, I would come to the Maribyrnong. Then all I had to do was turn right and keep going. Or so I thought.

The river bends lost me. The curves were so lugubrious and the trail so badly marked that I rode off into some suburban streets looking for a short cut but, arriving at roads which only seemed to go in circles, I was forced to retrace my pedalling all the way back to the river and set off again along its other bank. I texted Sosi to tell her I would be a little late, and drank some water. I felt like an idiot to have set off this way, but I also knew I had to keep going. I felt a little like an explorer, the suburbs my desert or my jungle. As I went on, the river, tranquil as a pond, began to sink between tired cliffs, pushing the houses on either side further and further apart, opening up a hollow on the city's face. My bike path left the riverside and took off up a hill in zigzags. I passed a jogger. This must have been an old section of the path, I thought, the council saving money. The path skated along the edge of some quiet suburb high on a hill. Below and beyond I could see the river falling deeper into the ancient gorges of the City of Brimbank. It must have been now a couple of kilometres across the top, from the backyard fences teetering on this side to the distant cul de sacs on the other.

Surveying my wilderness, contemplating the depths of its greying nooks and crannies, which at once lured and concerned me, and mindful of Sosina waiting for me patiently, sipping her Ethiopian coffee and watching Youtube (as she liked to do), I set off sideways. Leaving the ponderous security of the river, I would seek a faster, more direct route, hacking straight across the 'burbs. How could that fail? The sun was shining. Even without a compass I could trust myself with a reasonable sense of direction. I would find a long, stinky road that would cut through this landscape like a knife, sacrificing peace and nature for the slipstream of a bus.

It was the sort of *Boy's Own* adventure decision, it occurred to me in passing, that, for instance, Henry Morton Stanley ('Dr Livingstone, I presume') would have been making constantly in Central Africa back in the 1870s, weighing up whether to fight his way through the cliffs and rapids of the river or to beat a circuit through the jungle instead, as he ventured forth to meet some fabled African queen. I had been reading about Stanley's exploits in the context of the 'scramble for Africa', in which the continent and its resources were carved up by the European powers for their own enrichment. Stanley was a writer, too; he published vivid best-selling chronicles in which he described how he punished African communities who resisted his advances 'with the power of a father punishing a stubborn and disobedient son'. In one particular case, according to his own account, he achieved the fatherly murder of thirty-three locals and then 'proceeded along the coast [of the lake] paddling to the sound of sonorous drums and the cheering tones of the bugle, the English, American and Zanzibar flags flying gaily in union with a most animating scene.' Such, I reflected, was the tasteful civilising influence of my European forebears.

And I wondered – how could any father want to punish a son so violently?

I turned my back on the Maribyrnong. A promising road led due north and met another, slicing west. I was somewhere beyond Essendon. If I tacked like this, west and north, I would soon arrive at Sosi's. But I came to another junction, and with the hubris of a foreigner, decided another short cut was in order. Yes, the main road went north again; but, surely, my instincts told me, at this point that would be taking me further than I needed to travel in that direction. Ahead, in the backstreets, I would find the long-dreamt-of (by me, at least) north-west track to St Albans. After a while the road ran out, I saw, but I could pitch across country through some dirtlands above the distant river. Now I could see, amidst the abyss, the distant ruins of a high railway bridge dipping its delicate feet, like a wading bird, into the gorge. And beyond that, a newer bridge, the Ted Whitten, named for the greatest footballer ever to play for Footscray. I knew I had to reach and cross that bridge, because Sosi lived close by on the other side. It was tempting to try to put my bike across my shoulders and walk into the wilderness straight towards Ted Whitten. Ted himself probably would have been strong enough to do such a thing but my panniers were very heavy. I had my laptop.

I found a road licking to the right. I was in the 1980s now, town planning–wise. Every little road was curved. I took this one, that one, this one, closer, closer, until I came to a street that ran stubbornly sideways to the northeast, with no streets cutting through it, in the direction I was after. I felt like a lab rat stuck in an experiment, pedalling back and forth along this street searching for an exit. What was going on here? Then I noticed the high embankment steeped behind the houses. Fuck. The Western Ring Road! From the back it was a long, curved levee, an impenetrable bastion, a banal engineering marvel. I almost cried. I gave up on my vision of the undiscovered path. I accepted that I did not know better than the landscape. I accepted that I would be extremely late. I accepted that there could be worse things. I limped, in so far as a cyclist can limp, back to the main road I had disdained fifteen minutes earlier. *A wise man stays on the path where many have travelled*, a voice told me. A smarmy, told-you-so voice. Murderous Stanley wouldn't have listened to such a voice. But, for that matter, Sosi wouldn't have listened to such a voice either. So I took it with a grain of salt.

On subsequent trips to Sosi's house, I put my bike on the train to St Albans station and rode from there, a neat kilometre.

One day, only a week after the fifteen first arrived at the house on Somerville Road, one of the Ethiopian circus boys, Hassan, who had found a bike and taken to riding it here and there, came face to face with two men in a car. They were, unmistakably, Gizaw, the Circus Ethiopia tour manager, and Joske, its European agent and organiser of the Australian tour, evidently searching the streets of Melbourne's West to find the fifteen who had fled. Frightened out of his wits, Hassan turned his bicycle around, raced home to the big house and shut the door. Gizaw and Joske followed in their car.

A knock came on the door.

One of the fifteen opened it.

'Hello,' said Gizaw and Joske smiling, as if nothing had happened.

One or possibly all of the fifteen closed the door again. They were scared this meant everything was now finished for them in Australia. How much power did the men outside have? Had they been talking with the Immigration Department? The police?

Some adults from the local Ethiopian community happened to be in the house, says Sosi. 'These adults told us: this is Australia; unless they have a court order or you give them permission to come into the house, they are not allowed to enter.'

The door stayed shut.

Outside on the front verandah Gizaw started talking through the door.

'Look,' he said, 'all we want to do is talk to you. I think the decision you made is wrong and I think you should come back. I know most of you don't want to do this; it's going to hurt the circus; it's going to hurt the country. You have to come back – this is wrong; you're very young. But lets just talk about it...'

Sosi had her ear to the door. Fifteen pairs of ears were nearby. Inside the house there was now a big discussion. Should we let them in or not? Some said no, but Sosi fell towards yes. She still respected Gizaw and Joske; they had helped her out and taken her around the world. She felt it would be rude only a week later to leave them out on the verandah. She wanted to hear what they would say. She knew they couldn't drag the fifteen from the house: this was Australia.

They were let in, and invited to sit on a couch in the lounge room. Everyone congregated in a circle around them. Some were standing, some sitting on the floor. Joske launched into the speech I suppose he had been thinking about all week, Gizaw translating into Amharic:

'Look,' said Joske, 'the tour has only just begun, you know. It is four months long; we have a very exciting time in Europe ahead of us. And I know,' he said, and repeated for emphasis, 'I know, *I know* it is a very wrong decision you have made. We can fix the problems, we can fix up what's happened in the circus, but to do that you need to come back. If you don't come back it's going to be very difficult to fix because the rest of the kids will be very disturbed...'

Everyone in the room was on edge. One of the older boys could not restrain his anger.

'What do you care about us?' he said. 'You don't know any-thing about what's happening in Ethiopia in the circus. You're in Europe! Why don't you leave us alone. We will make our own decisions.'

Joske, probably sensing he wasn't doing well, stood up as if to leave but instead walked over to Sosina. 'He wanted to talk to me in private,' she says. 'He knew me best of all because I had taught myself to speak pretty good English across all those years in Circus Ethiopia and when he had come to Ethiopia I had explained to him a lot of things about the culture and the country.'

She didn't want to talk with him in private because all the others wouldn't trust her any more. So she sat where she was on the floor and he came over to hold her hand and give her a big hug, and he said to her in English, with all of the others sitting around listening and watching, he said only to her: 'Sosina, do you want to stay here or do you want to come with us? Because I know for a fact that you've got a great future ahead of you and I don't want you to be stuck here and be a refugee. I don't want you to be in this situation. I think you can do everything you want to without staying here and I can help you with that.'

Some of the other kids couldn't understand very well but others knew exactly what he was saying to her.

'You have a great future, Sosina, and I can help you with your career if you want,'...and on and on.

And she, nervous, more nervous than as a cigarette seller talking with the manager of the St George brewery, more nervous than slipping into the unknown Sydney streets, and almost but not quite crying, said: 'I'm sorry, Joske, I'm really, really sorry for what happened, but when I put myself into this situation I knew what was happening and I know for a fact that I will never look back. I have rung my mother and told her I'm not going back. It's a decision that I have made personally and it's a decision that all the others have made, too, in their own minds, not to go back. So I'm very sorry but this is the situation.'

She says: 'I just tried to explain it to him.'

Then he got up and walked out. Gizaw, too.

Joske was still angry years later, according to Sosi. 'A long time after, he came to see Circus Oz in England when we were on tour there,' she says. 'He didn't talk to me.'

I have Sosina's voice with me, and the cicadas, as I write this. As usual, I recorded our latest round of conversations on my phone.

I listen to her voice and my voice (although it's mostly her voice) and the sound of the coffee cups chinking, the paper bags scrunching as we extract and pick apart the croissants (plain or almond) I have collected from the Vietnamese bakery in St Albans (I drive the car now to her house).

She highlighted all the bits in the draft I'd written that she thought we needed to discuss. I loved that, working through methodically. On the recordings you can hear the sound of turning pages, sometimes. 'This bit's fine, that bit's fine.' Every now and then she'll say: 'I like this part!' I always put a mark against those sections, a double tick, possibly three ticks if I think she's really keen.

She likes it when I'm honest.

A lot of people helped the fifteen. They got free food from something Sosi calls the Food Bank. Every Saturday a truck would come and take them to the Food Bank, where they could pick up anything they liked: tins and packages of food people had donated. One room in their house in Somerville Road was full of food. They stacked it in there from the truck. Anything you wanted, you could go into that room for it. Some things might be close to their use-by date. That was alright. That stuff was fine to eat.

The younger kids, under sixteen, were eligible for a youth allowance from the government, Centrelink. With this money coming in they could buy milk, bread and eggs. The rest of their food they gathered in the truck and stacked up in the food room.

Fifteen children and young adults crammed together in a small house with not a lot to do. The trampoline outside the kitchen window: bouncing, bouncing. The 1998 World Cup on the telly. They had two lounge rooms. One was the World Cup lounge room, full of screaming boys. Ricky Martin singing at the top of his voice: 'Go, go, go, Olé, olé, olé!' If you wanted to escape from the World Cup you went to the other lounge room, the electronic-organ-playing-loudly room. It was either World Cup or organ music.

The younger kids, up to and including Sosi, started going to the local school, Maribyrnong High, and became something of a sensation in the district. They all had bags of physical tricks and needed scant provocation to display them. No provocation, in fact. The phone at the house (local calls only) rang constantly. Local girls quickly came to the conclusion: these new African guys were hot. Sosi remembers how girls would turn up on the doorstep while the boys were on the phone to other girls who would soon be on the doorstep, too.

The first share house I lived in, in Adelaide, there were eight of us. That was far too many. It was a large house and some of the inhabitants I only met a few times over several months, scuttling through the kitchen.

But fifteen?

Fifteen kids. The World Cup 24/7. Someone playing organ loudly, someone on the phone. Someone on the doorstep, one room stacked high with decaying food and tin cans. The trampoline, bouncing, bouncing.

Who slept where? Were there any couples? Thinking about, you know, privacy. 'No, we would sleep in different places,' she said, 'There were lots of beds. *It was a church house.*' – as if this explains it – 'Some nights you would end up in this room because you were talking to so and so, or because it was warmer, or you would end up kipped on the lounge room floor when the TV couldn't keep you awake any longer. In Ethiopia we were used to sleeping overnight sometimes in a big hall at the circus, on a long strip of mat; everyone just slept wherever.'

In Ethiopia life is more communal, to this day. But – fifteen kids who'd never lived away from home before apart from on tour, thirteen of them boys and therefore if anything less domesticated. Abbiy, the eldest boy, organised a roster for cooking and cleaning. The younger boys checked the roster and ran away when it was their turn.

Some of them were not only lazy but highly inexperienced. Sosi remembers one boy, who will remain nameless, cooking rice for the first time in his life. Nobody had ever seen fit to tell him, or he hadn't been paying attention (possibly preoccupied with bouncing on the trampoline or improving his English on the phone or on the doorstep), but in any case he had not grasped the fact that rice expands substantially when boiled in water. He had what looked like a good quantity of rice in a saucepan, with what looked like a good quantity of water, in between drowning and dry, when the rice began to grow alarmingly. He added more water, and more again, but each time this only seemed to encourage the rice to grow more, until he was no longer shocked at the growing of the rice but concerned at the shrinking of the pot. As the slurry overflowed he transferred half into a second pot and proceeded with the two pots bubbling and expanding side by side, like a scene in a fairy tale. As he looked from one to the other it seemed to be a race between them as to which would reach the top first, and he began to think about the inevitable necessity of a third pot. Luckily for him, the rice was cooked before this next stage of the catastrophe was triggered. The household contemplated this vast supply of steaming rice.

The trampoline, bouncing, bouncing.

I used to bounce on a trampoline for hours, myself. For a time, every day after school when I was about thirteen, I would walk two doors down the street in Perth and bounce on the neighbours' trampoline, either by myself or with one of their children, who were younger than me. I loved my basic, repetitive, safe trampolining. Feet, knees, feet, backside. My best trick (there is always one) went like this: I would bounce on my backside with my feet stretched out in front, and then swivel 180 degrees in midair so as to land on my backside facing in the opposite direction. There wasn't really a name for this trick but, humble as it was, I practised it for hours. I can still feel the memory of its pleasure in my body.

But I never learnt advanced trampolining tricks because, unlike Sosi, I could never trust that my body would reappear intact and pain-free on the other side of a somersault. Other things I have not been able to do yet: tumble turns in swimming, also diving. They all involve a leap of faith. They all involve my head disappearing blindly into space, trusting that the world is still there: gravity, the surface of the pool, et cetera. To me, they are mole-like activities. I would be quite happy to do them if I had eyes at the top of my head. Otherwise, surely, it's like a plane flying with its cockpit positioned underneath and the pilot gazing stupidly at the ground and hoping for the best. Who would step into such a vehicle? Sosi would say to me: 'You get used to it; your body gets a sense of itself, knows where it is in the air. You learn the technique; how to tuck your neck in, tuck your knees up, or whatever it might be.'

But I think: *What about the first time? How do you make that leap?* Writing is not all that different.

Perhaps, I'm thinking, *I might learn tumble turns, at least.*

Light streamed in from the south into the newly opened back room at the Dancing Dog café where Sosi and I sat once again on 1950s-style tall-backed chairs encircling a coffee table. She was laughing about the days at Somerville Road. 'Some local Ethiopian ladies came to visit us,' she said. 'They looked at me and Sadra, the two girls. They said, *You girls! You have to do something about your hair! You have grown up now; you have to have your hair looking good.* They took us back to their flats in Ascot Vale, where there was a lady expert in hair. They took us to have rollers put in. Overnight I pulled all the rollers out while I was sleeping. In the morning when I woke up all the rollers were on the ground. I said, *I don't like this; I'm not doing this.* My hair went straight out sideways again. Wild. I didn't care…'

'And all this time you were still waiting to hear about your cases?'

'All the time we were waiting for our letters to arrive—'

All the time Marc LaChance was busy at the circus back in Ethiopia. He was still fighting to survive, working to force the fifteen to return. He sent over a lot of information to influence the Immigration Department in their decision.

'After three months they came. Fifteen letters all at once, all exactly the same: *Your application for a refugee visa has been rejected.*'

Apparently, it was ruled that they had not proved persecution.

But no grounds were given in the letters. (That was normal.)

'You may appeal this decision within 28 days.

Otherwise you will become an illegal alien.'

You will be sent home.

Yours sincerely.

9

Becoming

Next time Sosina and I talk there has been a breakthrough with Tewabé's proposed medical care. A surgeon at Western Hospital has agreed to help with the operations necessary, and will write a letter of support to submit to the Immigration Department with Sosina's application for a Medical Visa to bring him to Australia. It is obvious how relieved she is. She feels confident that the visa might soon be within reach. 'Now,' she says, 'I can concentrate on raising all the money I will need.' It might be forty grand. Her sister Meski has taken a job four nights a week in a factory, packing peanuts and sultanas, to help raise the money. Meski, who Sosina managed to bring to Australia in the wake of her brother Abraham's death, who the Immigration Department approved in less than four months after refusing Abraham three times in six years. Meski can only work four nights a week because she is also studying English full time in the city (Sosi had told her that she shouldn't study it in

Footscray where all the other Ethiopian migrants go because she'd never meet anyone outside their community).

Mel is working full time at the flash IT firm now, driving an hour across the city every day. Unlike most local Ethiopian–Australians he has found a way to move on from driving taxis and working night shift in factories. He works in his own field of expertise: computer security. 'He's slimmed down,' remarks Sosi approvingly, 'He's not eating all that junk food you eat when you drive a taxi all night.'

The household, one has the sense, is fully focused on their task of saving money to bring Tewabé out for his operation. Sosi has odd jobs here and there, teaching, performing, developing shows, cooking for festivals and looking after Raeey until her full time gig with *The Burlesque Hour* starts in June.

'It's a very different culture here,' says Sosi. 'Growing up in Ethiopia you want your mum to be full of gold. As much as the parents invest in their children, the children also invest in their parents. A lot of Ethiopians will build a house for their parents before they build one for themselves, if they can afford it. In Ethiopia you can't rely on money or on the government; all you can rely on is people. Here, people build their own boundaries. Everyone is segregated in her own place. They say they don't want to have to rely on people but, the way I think, you've got to rely on people and then they can rely on you, too. In Ethiopia there is nothing, but people like to share. I reckon it works better.'

'I'm so torn,' she says. 'Now that I have a daughter—' I look at her '—I wish she could have my childhood, in a way.'

She wonders who her daughter will become. Whom or what she will take after. Who will be her idols? Who will be her Josephine?

Josephine Baker was the black American performer who took Paris by storm in the 1920s. *King Kong* introduced Josephine to

Sosina. In 2004 Sosina auditioned for the Peter Jackson movie remake and landed a cameo as a performer onstage in a New York club. You can see her in an early scene doing her upside-down juggling routine.

In the film's wardrobe and make-up rooms in Wellington, New Zealand, they set to work on Sosina and afterwards gathered around to admire their creation in the mirror. 'You look exactly like her!' they exclaimed.

'Who?'

'Josephine Baker!' And they passed across some photographs.

Josephine sits upon a bench, one arm draped across her tucked-up knees. Mouth puckered with lipstick like chocolate, she gazes past us, over her left shoulder. Her hair, cut short and lacquered to her head from a middle part so that her forehead forms a gable, descends into a perfect curl positioned on her cheek, a cup for catching tears, something lick-able. She wears a bikini top strung with beads and a faux-grass skirt trimmed with long slender leaves and giant beaded cobs of corn. Her fingers rest upon a ukelele by her shiny dance shoes. It is an artful studio pose, suggesting she could hop up and do a number at any moment.

Sosi wanted to know more about this woman. She fell immediately into deep Josephine Baker research; later on, I followed.

Josephine Baker welled up in the Parisian imagination, fully formed, in 1925. News of the opening night of *La Revue Négre* at the Théâtre des Champs-Élysées, in which a nineteen-year-old Baker stole the show, reverberated across the epicentre of the Western avant-garde. Léger, Picabia, Cocteau, Picasso, Robert Desnos, Louis Aragon, Alexander Calder: all were at the theatre or, wishing that they had been, sought out Baker afterwards. *La Revue Négre* was a concept show designed to stoke the Parisian fascination with all things 'Negro'. For the first time an entire African-American performing ensemble was recruited in New York and shipped across to Europe. Baker, a city slum girl from the American midwest, symbolised their fantasies of dark, mysterious, magnificently 'primitive' black Africa.

Africa, since the explorations and conquests of the nineteenth century, had occupied an increasingly complex and lurid space in the European and American unconscious. Black Africans, in a former time simply synonymous with slaves in the Christian mind, now featured in a more diverse set of fantasies. The epic tales of explorers like De Brazza and Stanley, from the 1860s onwards, penetrating in true White Man-ly style deep into the dank wet jungles of the Dark Continent, brought stories of naked spear-throwing savages and treacherous Swahili. Not to mention strange primitive artifacts: totems, sculptures, carvings – trophies for displaying and hoarding in the great metropolitan museums. Skulls and skeletons were studied, too, in the burgeoning European scientific community. Post-Darwin, we, suddenly, were close cousins with apes: naturally, it seemed, the primitives of Africa could form a neat stepping stone between the lower primates and civilised Salon Man.

Private zoos exhibiting exotic wild beasts captured in the new colonies soon featured exotic wild humans, too. Nubians, pygmies, Ethiops…they were oft times situated in the 'Primate House', most likely on display each afternoon. The 1889 Paris World Fair, designed to showcase all the marvels of the modern world, included, alongside the controversial new Eiffel Tower, a large *village negre* (Negro Village) through which visitors could wander, examining the specially imported natives as if strolling past living dioramas.

Around 1906, artists began to decipher a new contrasting meaning for all things African. Searching to break away from tired-out Western aesthetic traditions, as the new twentieth century seemed to call for, they discovered inspiration in the colonial exhibits of the Musée d'Ethnographie du Trocadéro and the second-hand stalls of the flea markets of Paris, encountering there the mystical strangeness of what they lumped together as *l'art negre*. For Picasso,

Matisse and many others, including those who formed Dada and Surrealism, masks and figures from black Africa signaled nothing less than a way to see the world anew, to encounter its unfiltered essence, to rip away the veneer of European bourgeois manners and pretension and uncover the authentic. All the high champions of Modernist art at this time and into the postwar era of the 1920s borrowed (or stole) heavily from 'Africa'.

So when Josephine arrived, Paris was hungry for her. *La Revue Négre* transported the white audience to a shocking, thrilling faraway place peopled entirely by blacks. Just as the audience had become accustomed to this scene, Baker appeared: frenetic, clowning, cross-eyed. Her biographer Phyllis Rose describes her at this moment as a 'weird cross between a kangaroo, a bicyclist, and a machine gun'. It is hard to imagine what that could produce but I suppose that is the point: her comedy and movement implied a liberation of what it meant to be a human, in our funny, awkward bodies.

Later in the show Josephine re-entered bare-breasted for her *danse sauvage*, wearing a skirt of feathers. She danced as nobody had ever been seen to dance before, in that city or that continent, shaking her hips and stomach and above all else her rear end violently, cataclysmically, so that audience members fled or whistled in disgust while others rose and cheered as her blast of unkempt sexuality caused all the long, straight boulevards of Paris, not to mention all the curving avenues, to shudder. She danced the Charleston. She danced what became known as her 'stomach dance'; she was compared to a panther, a snake, a giraffe. Finally, it was said that her arse quivered like a hummingbird.

Reviewers of the show, their senses overstimulated, their minds already stacked with Africana bric-a-brac and legend, scarcely knew where to start:

'We don't understand their language, we can't find a way to tie the scenes together, but everything we've ever read flashes across our enchanted minds: adventure novels, glimpses of enormous steam-boats swallowing up clusters of Negroes who carry rich burdens, a caterwauling woman in an unknown port…stories of missionaries and travellers…sacred dancers, the Sudan…plantation landscapes, the melancholy songs of Creole nurses, the Negro soul with its animal energy, its childish joys, the sad bygone time of slavery, we had all that listening to the singer with the jungle voice, admiring Louis Douglas's hectic skill…and the pretty coffee-coloured raga-muffin who is the star of the troupe, Josephine Baker.'

Sosina immediately recognised Josephine as her sister, her dance partner, her soul mate. She read on: how Josephine's stage career went from strength to strength, how she later had an affair with Frida Kahlo, assisted the French Resistance to the Nazis in North Africa, adopted a multiracial multinational brood of chil-dren and installed her family in a chateau in the south of France. In April 1975, fifty years after *La Revue Négre,* Josephine opened her final show, at the age of sixty-nine. This time the audience included Princess Grace, Mick Jagger, Sophia Loren and Jeanne Moreau. Josephine – the old trouper – changed costumes twelve times during the performance. The critics, for the most part, raved. Four days later she was dead. A stroke.

When I think of Josephine I see Sosina. I see them chatting together backstage, comparing notes, working up an act together.

When Sosina thinks of Josephine she *is* Josephine.

After *King Kong,* she began daydreaming of a new act she would do with Circus Oz, a fresh setting for her bounce ball-juggling routine. She would be Josephine from a few years after *La Revue Négre,* when she had acquired more power and sophistication in her shows. Sosi's take on Josephine was to flatten her hair down, wear a tailcoat and black stockings, and be carried onstage by three top-hatted (white) male dancers as the faux–Cotton Club band struck up a Charleston. The ascending steps in her bounce ball-juggling act, in which the physics of standard juggling is inverted and the balls are bounced onto the floor instead of thrown into the air – three balls, three balls upside down in a backbend, four balls through her legs, five balls rotating in a circle, six and finally seven balls all simultaneously suspended in trails and arcs between her fingers and the floor – are as if verses, between which she plays out satiric interludes of Josephine-dancing with her devoted chorus line.

Sosi's Josephine act became a hit in the Circus Oz show. Eventually they toured to New York City: the New Victory Theatre on 42nd Street. Sosi was nervous to be bringing her tribute to Josephine back to where Josephine herself had started on Broadway.

As she came offstage and all was well, the theatre's African-American wardrobe supervisor, Sharlon, who looked after the maintenance and washing of the stage clothes, was lit up: 'You know, you really remind of someone doing that routine!'

'Who? said Sosi.

And Sharlon said: 'Do you know Josephine Baker?'

The immigration cases of the fifteen Ethiopian asylum seekers dragged on through 1998 and 1999. After their initial rejection, they each lodged appeals to the Refugee Review Tribunal.

Members of the local Ethiopian community would come to the house at Somerville Road with advice and coaching on interviews at the Tribunal: *Don't be scared, don't rush your answers, think it through; if you don't understand the question you can ask for it to be repeated, because once you say something you can never pull it back again, that tape is running…don't be scared…*These people all had too much experience of their own with refugee processes, be it in Australia or in the camps of Kenya.

Meanwhile Sosi was learning English at Maribyrnong High School and thinking, thinking, what to do next.

In the distance, across the river and beyond the docks, at night she saw the lit-up furnace of the city. Skyscrapers like so many shiny pencils stuck deep into clay.

The nearby snaking train would take them there.

The house was thick with bodies, noise. Such a relief to step out into a quiet carriage of apprehensive football fans or teenage lovers with fingers interlaced. At the other end, Flinders Street. Sosi and companions leapt the ticket barriers and flowed into the city crowds. They weren't afraid of getting caught; they had no money, nothing that could be taken from them. (Later, clinging to citizenship, she would always buy a ticket.) Like Walter Benjamin's *flâneur*, they wandered the metropolis with no purpose other than to absorb sensation. Compared to Addis, all was condensed, heightened, spun and polished.

Swanston Street, that great tacky thoroughfare of Melbourne, split the city in two, its fast-food joints, its Asian cafés packed with homesick overseas students, its bitumen smeared with horseshit from the tourist carriages. In Flinders Lane the *flâneuse* listened to the clack of heels echoing off glass and stone; she gazed into the all-white eyes of mannequins with bumps for breasts and pointy elbows. Up Little Bourke Street, Chinatown, she found alleyways of restaurants and laughter converging until the crowd surged on to Russell Street. Suddenly, around the corner, the video game parlours and the junkies. She got used to being stared at.

Filled up with their new home, still hungry for its embrace, the band of anonymous Ethiopian teenagers leapt back across the ticket barriers, back into the suburbs and their temporary home, there to raid the fridge, fall asleep and dream of – what? Neon lights and chewing gum? Walking, walking. The freedom to walk anywhere.

First opportunity she got, Sosi jumped ship from Somerville Road. She and the other girl of the fifteen, Sabla, were invited by an Australian family who had adopted an Ethiopian baby to live rent-free in the bungalow in their backyard in exchange for babysitting the child three days a week. On the first day they encountered the mysteries of disposable nappies (nappies of any sort being unfamiliar to them, coming from Ethiopia) and the great stocks of shop-bought toys favoured by Australians.

The next step was to make some money. In immigration limbo, the kids relied totally on charities. Centrelink wouldn't give them payments if they were over eighteen. So one day Sosi found herself on Acland Street, the main drag of Melbourne's old seaside resort suburb of St Kilda. She had met a woman called Gemma who, to make some cash, read tarot cards on the street there, outside a hippie Asian shop. Sosi asked the shop if she could set herself up on a chair beside Gemma, and offer a hair-braiding service. It would be a 60/40 split her way. Six dollars per plait. Tight, African-style. She could do extensions, colours, beads. Pretty soon she was not doing too badly. She was fast with her hands. She charmed the customers. She had money in her pocket; just like selling cigarettes in Addis.

Sosi braided hair on Acland Street each weekend. Over summer she could go there four or five days a week, making thirty or thirty-five dollars a day. That was not bad, considering.

On Acland Street she watched the town promenading by. Dogs all cut and coloured, prettier than their owners.

She relied on Gemma for protection from her own naivety. Older men would come along and offer to take her out. They would say they had a cousin who needed her hair done and if she would just like to come back to their place she could do their cousin's hair and get paid a lot of money. And Sosina would chat with them politely, because she had been brought up to respect her elders, and in Ethiopia one always talks to strangers. But Gemma, much older and wiser in the ways of Acland Street, would say: 'FUCK OFF!' to the old men, and then to Sosina, 'You don't know these people; don't talk to them; you can't trust them...'

One time a young Filipina–Australian girl, barely Sosi's age, came by with a husband old enough to be her grandfather. The girl watched Sosi braiding; her husband would pay for anything she wanted. She offered Sosi $350 to come to her house and do a full plait of her hair with extensions, eight hours' worth. This time Gemma gave the nod: safe to go.

They picked Sosina up from Acland Street and drove her to their house in a nearby suburb. For eight hours, the husband left the two women alone to plait and talk.

The house was like a small palace, suburban style. Sosina, plaiting, plied the girl with questions. Like Josephine Baker but in a more sombre hue, this girl was an alternative version of herself.

The husband had bought her, brought her from the Philippines. Her parents had told her she had no choice; it was the only chance they had to improve the circumstances of the family as a whole. She must be exported to the rich world and could afterwards send back cash courtesy of this wealthy man who wanted to possess her in his final years. It was and is a not-uncommon strategy, the contemporary version of an age-old tale of the forced bartering of the beautiful young woman. She left behind a boyfriend in the Philippines but now, she told Sosina, she loved her husband. He took her out to the casino on his arm, he bought her expensive jewellery – *This diamond, and this one, too, see?*

'What do you do all day,' asked Sosina?

'I clean up the house.' (It was spotless.) 'I cook very good meals. I wait for my husband to come home.'

Her only friends were other girls like her: young, Filipina, waiting in their suburban palaces for their husbands to come home. Waiting for their husbands one day soon to die. This loneliness, their only ticket out.

Sosina, who had no papers yet, no guarantee of anything in this country, returned to her piece of footpath on Acland Street. She breathed in the car-fumed smell of freedom.

10

The things we learn

The teachers at Maribyrnong High School were impressed that Sosina could perform quadratic equations with her hands. Virtually no school kid had a calculator in Ethiopia when Sosina was growing up, so she didn't view this as a particularly outstanding talent. Any smart kid could perform equations with their hands. In Ethiopia you had your books, your pen, pencil and eraser. If you could afford it, a ruler and a compass. If not, you borrowed them from the person next to you, or opposite.

It wasn't only the equations; they said her English was improving all the time. They reckoned she didn't need to hang around another year to do her final high school exams. She could move directly into higher (vocational) education.

On Acland Street, Sosina had met a photographer named Suzanne who told her she had a beautiful face and beautiful hair and should call the number on her business card if she would like to have photographs taken. Four months later Suzanne came by again and asked Sosina why she hadn't called, to which she had no good answer and, by the way, was now very much inclined to have her photograph taken by this woman who looked like she knew exactly what she was doing. Having one's photograph taken, after all, is a kind of performance; involving costumes, make-up, acting.

Sosi, in Suzanne's house. Sosi, on St Kilda Beach.

To this day, both Suzanne and Sosina love these photographs.

Afterwards, it occurred to Sosina to ask Suzanne how to find a course she could enrol in: theatre or circus, because that was what she loved.

Suzanne brought a whole bunch of flyers and spread them out. Together they found one offered by Swinburne University called an Advanced Diploma in Theatre, Small Companies. Sosi decided that this would be the one.

Suzanne kindly offered to make the call for Sosi. The very nice woman on the other end of the line informed her that, since it was February, enrolments for that year had already closed, unfortunately. There was absolutely nothing that could be done other than to apply in November for the following year's program.

This is the point at which I, good boy, would have stopped. I, good boy, would have thought, *What a shame but, after all, I suppose the rules are very clear and can't be varied just to suit me because rules, after all, are rules, and what would happen if all the rules started to be varied to suit me or you or someone else.* About now my mother's voice would chime in — as it did in the car driving away from the police station from which she had retrieved me following the green–illegal–substance incident back when I was seventeen — saying, 'I *know* people say that (green illegal substance) is no better or worse than alcohol but it *is* against the law so that means you just can't *ever* take it.' Forlornly, pleading.

Okay, so I'm not entirely a good boy. I strayed around the fringes.

But I come from a family of earnest, law-abiding types. Middle-class public servants, teachers. Only my great uncle, Uncle Ben, broke the mold as an adventurer, with three wives, a foul mouth and a World War II amphibious jeep he customised in a New England garage. Uncle Ben set off in 1953 with his third wife into the ocean east from New York City, only to return three years later having passed through Morocco, Paris, Istanbul, Calcutta, Alaska and selected points in between, bearing many stories but minus (can you blame her) the third wife. (As the jacket of the book so elegantly describes it: *Eleanor stepped down in Calcutta.*) Sosina is exactly like Uncle Ben: unafraid to swim out into unknown waters. He, driving his jeep down the middle of the Hudson River as if it were a country lane, regarded the Queen Mary not as a crushing weight above him but a photo opportunity. She, juggling eight balls, two continents, the first world and the third, the welfare of her entire extended family and her ever-expanding showbiz career.

This is the point at which Sosina called the university again.

'You rang just before?' said the (nice) woman on the other end. 'We told you. It's too late this year. Sorry.' Hung up.

And this is the point at which Sosina got on a train, leaping over the ticket barrier as usual, and dispatched herself to the Swinburne campus in Prahran.

(By now my middle-class mug would have been under the table, if there had been one, in embarrassment.)

Finding the correct office, she came face to face with the (still nice, in principle) woman, the administrator.

'I want to talk to John Butler,' said Sosina, knowing from her research that John Butler ran the course.

'Do you have an appointment with John?'

'No.'

Sosina stood there with her big eyes, until the woman abandoned her resistance: 'I'll see what I can do.'

She rang John Butler and said: 'The girl who rang, she's here.'

A little while later, he appeared.

'Can I help you?'

'I want to be in this course.'

'Yes, but we've told you, you're too late. Applications closed before Christmas.'

He was nice about it, too.

But Sosina had her foot wedged firmly in the door.

'I'll be very good in that course, you know. I came here to this country in a travelling circus. I'm a performer. I've travelled around. Adelaide, Denmark, Germany, about sixteen countries. I've done performing but, you know, what I want is to learn all the other aspects, the lights, the sounds and stuff. Because I've always been onstage, I want to understand these other things...'

She took a breath.

Already, perhaps, he had begun to change his mind. This girl: surely she took him back to his love of acrobatics, to the Nanjing Project he participated in several years before in which Chinese acrobats came to Australia for several months to train young locals and transformed the Australian circus scene?

'Do you have permanent residency?'

'No, I am applying for that.'

'That will be a big problem.'

'Why?'

'If you were accepted, we would have to consider you as an international student.'

'What does that mean?'

'You have to pay ten thousand dollars a year, up front.'

Ten thousand dollars. Sosina didn't even have ten cents in her pocket. She had jumped the train.

She explained this.

He put up his arms.

'These are the regulations; that's how it works. I can't personally give you special permission.'

'It can't happen in this country.'

'It's impossible.'

In front of him, though he didn't realise it, stood the scrawny cigarette seller with the afro and the made-up karate moves.

'You know what,' she said finally: 'if you just give me the spot, I will find the money.'

'Give you the spot?'

'Give me an audition. I will find the money.'

As she said this she had no idea what she was talking about. How would she find ten thousand dollars? But she glared at him as if there was nothing surer in the world.

She didn't budge.

That afternoon he organised an audition and an interview. Dragged along two colleagues.

'What if a famous circus comes along, Circus Oz or Cirque du Soleil, and says to you, Sosina, run away and join our circus. What are you going to say?'

The cigarette seller was smart enough for this one.

'I'm going to say that I don't want to go because I want to do this course. I've done a lot of travelling already. I want to learn the other aspects of performing.'

She stood up and stretched.

'Shall I do something?'

(What exactly did you do, Sosina?)

An updated version of her lounge room act, her playground act. Or, as she tosses out the memory:

'Bit of African dance, bit of flip-flap, a few things...'

(Precisely the routine Josephine Baker would have done in the same situation.)

'Flip-flap?'

'Yeah, bit of tumbling…and they said: *Okay, you're in.*'

She just needed the money.

On the way home, at the ticket barrier, the leap effortless. All the way to Footscray.

Next morning, Sosina was at the door of the Red Cross down in City Road, South Melbourne. She knew a woman there called Lucy who had helped the fifteen asylum seekers, bringing them clothes and books.

Sosi explained her situation.

'I want to go to study but they are asking for ten thousand dollars.'

She started to cry.

Lucy sympathised: 'Oh, dear. That's very hard.'

Through tears, Sosina continued, with the desperation of someone who is cornered: 'You don't want to see me on the street, right? You don't want to see me doing bad things. I want to go to school, that's all I want.'

This was all true.

At this point, according to Sosina, Lucy began to grow very anxious about her plight. She said: 'Don't worry, I'll see what I can do.'

After three days on the telephone, Lucy called Sosina. 'The Carlton Rotary Club is happy to offer you a scholarship.'

The impossible made possible. People will help each other where they can.

From the drawer in Lucy's desk emerged all the supplies Sosi needed to begin her tertiary education. Exercise books. Pens. Paper. (A calculator still wouldn't be required.)

'Now go to school,' said Lucy.

By this time, although Sosi and the other fourteen who had fled together to this foreign place were still in immigration limbo, with either their first or second rejection letter flapping in their faces, they were at least granted work permits.

The younger ones were still at high school but the others, with the exception of Sosina, took up whatever work that they could find. This meant factory jobs. If you were lucky, like Mel, it was a furniture factory, making chairs and tables. For the rest it was the peanut factory, packing boxes, part of the assembly line machine. The standard immigrant story, taking the shit jobs the locals could disdain.

Sosina thought: *If I'm going to be sent back, would I rather have money or knowledge?* She preferred to braid hair on the street and go to university.

The Red Cross helped them find longer-term accommodation. They split up into small groups and lived in Housing Commission flats across the city. This left Sosina free to do her own thing.

Her own thing, which was many things.

In the daytime: university. Where all the other students, fresh from high school, chattered away in incomprehensible Australian accents. Still living at home with their parents, their concerns seemed bizarrely trivial. 'I was *so angry* with my mother…'

Sosi listened to them at lunchtime. She offered around her food to share. They shrank back as if the cholera and typhoid was visible for all to see.

'That's *your* lunch, Sosina,' they said.

She said: 'I know it's my lunch. I packed it myself.'

'We all eat our own food here. Separately.'

They might have allergies or reactions. They had learnt since childcare that everyone has his or her own bowl. They were happy to educate this African refugee girl into the advanced intricacies of the modern world. Like lunch-wrap and individual yoghurt tubs.

'Do you have television in Ethiopia? Do you live in, like, those little bamboo huts? Straw huts?'

'Yes. And you know what?'

'What?'

Six or eight or ten of them pressed in around her, well-scrubbed shiny white kids.

She whispered: 'I have a pet lion. And pet elephants.'

'Really?!'

'Really.'

'Really?'

They would all go home and tell their parents this. They would all go out and tell their friends.

Sosina looked around at their innocent protected faces.

'You must be crazy to believe that! You really believe I have pet elephants?'

Now they were hurt.

'Well, how are we to know?'

'You need to go out into the world!' Sosina scolded them. 'You need to travel, read up.'

At night she found a place to train, to hone her circus skills. She fell in with a group of young people training at a gymnastics club. Former gymnasts with dreams of circus. She bonded with them over hours shared on the sprung floor, beam and parallel bars. These became her first Australian group of friends. From them she learnt essential local rituals like going to the pub after work and hanging out at the beach or picnicking at St Kilda.

Around the corner from the university, just off boutique-lined inner-city Chapel Street, Prahran, Sosi noticed a shop called *Afrikeko*. A hairdresser specialising in African-style dreadlocks and braiding. She went inside and told the shop-owner that, if she ever needed a hair-braider, she, Sosina, could do the job very well and very fast. In fact, as it turned out, she could do the job much better than the shop-owner herself, whose name was Laurie, and she could do it much, much better than the unreliable and soon-to-be-former employee Carlos. Carlos and Laurie had developed a technique of braiding together, two sides of the same head, in unison. Assessing Laurie's expertise at braiding, or relative lack thereof, Sosina proposed a new deal. She would do all the braiding by herself and do it just as fast: it would look perfect and the customers would be satisfied. She would take 70 per cent of the price in cash. In one day she could complete what Laurie and Carlos between them had managed, but make it look a whole lot better. She would entertain the clients with circus stories. What's more, when she saw the prices charged for hair accessories, she realised it made sense to bring her own hair extensions, sourced from cheaper suppliers in Footscray, and her own hairspray, likewise sourced, and to sell them at a south-of-the-river mark-up on the side. For a day's work each Saturday she would make $400 in her hand.

Laurie soon offered Sosina more days a week, as the customers were lining up. However, one day a week was plenty; $400 was plenty. There were too many other things she had on.

Saturdays in Chapel Street became an education in itself, in the ways of the world. In between and over the heads of customers, Laurie and Sosina chatted all day long. Laurie's regulars would come in and tell her all about the latest dramas in their love life, and she in her high boots and lashings of mascara would soothe and comfort them, or offer sage advice. About lunchtime Laurie would open the front door a crack and poke her hand outside to feel if the day was hot or cold.

Sosi's best friend at the Small Companies course at university was a boy called Robert. When her latest rejection letter came from Immigration and she cried in front of Robert, he wept along with her, holding her hand. To cheer her up, he stood up and performed several Indian dances. He was learning them in evening classes. It made her laugh.

Robert proved able to empathise with Sosina in a way she found hard to reciprocate at first.

One day she came across him crying.

'My boyfriend — I broke up with him. He doesn't love me any more.'

His reaction appeared to be out of all proportion.

'That's alright. You can have other boyfriends.'

'Yes, but he has hurt me so much.' said Robert, stressing the pinprick-pain of every word.

Overboard. He was going.

'Why do you care so much?' (She was trying to be helpful.) 'Don't worry about it!' (Petty arguments and squabbles. Friends were always having these.)

But he went on and on, shivering and snivelling.

She really wanted to help him if she could.

'Why'd you break up?'

'I saw him making love to someone else, in my house. I found him making love to someone else.'

This was the most confusing thing he'd said so far. Why — did — he — care?

He spelt it out.

'He was sleeping with this guy!'

As if in a cartoon, Sosi's whole face opened out into a cheap amazed copy of Edvard Munch's *The Scream*.

'Wow! Your friend is gay! Was he always gay?'

'What do you mean?'

'Has he always been gay?'

Before he could think of anything to reply to this, she, who had already developed a far more open mind in these matters than the average Ethiopian, continued, almost scolding:

'I don't think you should break up with him because of that. That's his choice, you know.'

About now, she was feeling like just about the most sophisticated nineteen-year-old girl ever to step out of Addis Ababa.

'Sosi,' explained Robert, 'He's my boyfriend. We sleep together. We *sleep* together!'

And since even this had not yet done the job: 'He – is – my – sexual – partner.'

She leant back and regarded the evidence of her own blindness. 'You're – GAY.'

'Yes.'

It was so obvious. They both laughed.

Things *are* so obvious in retrospect. Sosi tells many stories like this one, against herself. It is hard to underestimate how difficult it is to take on another culture, to embrace, even understand, its nuances and norms. Sexual relations in Ethiopia, so far as Sosi knew, were between a man and a woman. Homosexuality wasn't even a category, much less a valid one.

Becoming friends with Robert, and meeting the regulars of *Afrikeko*, Sosi discovered how many different threads of desire were possible, and that Marc LaChance was the exception not the rule among those who deviate from sexual norms.

There was Gary from across the road; he would come into *Afrikeko* once a week to have his hair washed. He had pots of money and several boyfriends on the go, one or other of which would this week or tomorrow break his heart.

'Be gentle. Be gentle!' he would say to her. He insisted on only the softest washing of his hair. His greatest fear was baldness. Hairs yanked, tumbling, willy-nilly. Next thing: in the mirror, sad old man. Boyfriendless forever.

Meanwhile, Laurie was a font of reliable information.

'Laurie,' said Sosina, 'I've got a friend at uni. He told me he's working in a bath-house. Massage. He makes heaps of money, doing *happy endings*. What's a *happy ending*?'

Or: 'Laurie, that lady in Chapel Street, the one who walks up and down in the black latex and stilettos. What's she doing walking around with a whip? Whips in Ethiopia are for animals in the countryside. Why does she need that whip in Chapel Street?'

Or: 'Laurie, those two guys, those customers just now – what were they talking about? Going to that park in Chapel Street?'

'Yes, Sosina, they go to the park at night and have sex in the darkness with total strangers. That's what they love to do more than anything.'

Sosi, thinking all the time: *Wow! What next?* Going back to see her friends who arrived here in Australia with her, sheltered in the bosom of the Ethiopian community of Footscray. They wouldn't even begin to understand the uses whips were put to every day on Chapel Street.

At the same time as Sosi is telling me these stories I find myself, by way of contrast, poring over books of Ethiopian history. These stories, too, swirl with rumour and embellishment.

Ethiopia has always occupied a special place on the margins of the Western mind. At or beyond the boundaries of the known world lived the Ethiops, black-skinned descendants of Noah, it was claimed. A great Christian empire grew up at Axum in the fourth century AD. The town is still there, a faintly touristed shadow of its former self, several hundred kilometres north of Addis Ababa. Coins bearing the heads of twenty-four different kings from this time have been discovered by archaeologists. One of these emperors, Kaleb, was famous for sailing across the Red Sea and establishing a colony in Arabia. Historians and emissaries from the Greek and Roman worlds visited Axum and brought back their chronicles, and a mission was established in Jerusalem to represent the Ethiopian church.

Later, as with many things in the Dark Ages, much of this was forgotten. Sketchy tales emerged in Europe in the twelfth century of a magnificent far-off kingdom ruled by a Christian priest-king named Prester John. Prester John was first thought to abide somewhere in the vicinity of India, but this estimate was later re-jigged to Ethiopia (India and Ethiopia were thought to be separated only by a narrow strait, so this confusion was understandable).

Prester John was, for centuries, a beacon of Christian hope somewhere on the far side of barbarism and ungodliness, the endless deserts and the jungles. If only he could be reached! In desperation, the Pope wrote a letter to Prester John in 1177, attempting to enlist his support in the never-ending Crusades against the Saracens of the Eastern Sultanates. One can only imagine the fate of the hapless messenger dispatched with the task of delivering this mail.

Prester John, it was said, had the power of cutting off the flow of the Nile into Egypt (a fear that persists to this day). He lived, perhaps, by the Mountains of the Moon, where the source of the Nile was known to be beyond reach.

In the country of Prester John, children were baptised with fire instead of water. Presumably, this explained the colour of their skin.

In the wake of the Enlightenment, books such as S. Augustus Mitchell's *Ancient Geography, designed for Academies, Schools and Families, a System of Classical and Sacred Geography, embellished with Engravings of Remarkable Events, Views of Ancient Cities and Various Interesting Antique Remains, together with an Ancient Atlas, containing Maps illustrating the Work*, published in Philadelphia in 1852, brought what at that time passed as the latest knowledge in geography and history to their readers. Now they read more like fantasies. Speaking of Ethiopia (which merits a page and a half), Mitchell briefly mentions Axum and obelisks 'like those of Egypt' before plunging in to the juicy stuff:

'Among the rude tribes in this part of Africa, some lived on locusts, and some on the flesh of elephants and ostriches; the last two were called Elephantoph'agi, and Struthoph'agi. The Troglod'ytes, a race of rude shepherds, lived in caves. The Blem'myes were fabled to be without heads, and to have their eyes and mouths in their breasts. The Pyg'mies were a nation of dwarfs, who warred with the cranes, and went to battle mounted on the backs of goats and rams. Recent travellers in this part of Africa state that the inhabitants report a nation of diminutive stature as still resident in the interior.'

'The Macro'bii (long-lived), one of the most noted Ethiopian nations, resided south of Mer'oe. These people are described as a handsome and vigorous race: they elected the tallest among them to be king. The age of one hundred and twenty years, and even upwards, was not uncommon among them; hence their name.'

Imagine the white American, British or Australian schoolchildren (my ancestors), listening to this, following with their fingers across the pages – how these monstrous tribes of Ethiopia must have slipped into their dreams. And, moreover, slipped like a veil, without memory or trace, across the faces of any black people they encountered: those their elders, if polite, called *negroes, natives*... These fantasies and fears, which now seem ludicrous, nevertheless remain, buried deep in the bedrock of my culture. It is such racial associations that racism, whether it be subtle or savage, taps into.

Golliwogs. When we laugh uneasily and say it's 'not PC' to talk about golliwogs anymore, it's because we know that just censoring the word does not take away the cultural baggage that came with it.

I have always loved geography. Atlases, encyclopaedias. When I was four my sole-parenting mother left me in the house of Nanny Neale while she went off to work. Nanny Neale had a set of encyclopaedias I was allowed to open on the lounge room floor. The curtains, in my memory, were always closed against the summer heat, and I sat cross-legged, the heavy book across my lap. I couldn't read yet so I went directly to the colour plates. There they were, my friends, the wild beasts of Africa, the animal kingdom's all-time greatest hits. (No sign of the people.)

The Ethiopians themselves, or at least their ruling classes, developed over centuries their own imperial myths and legends. A text believed to have been compiled in the 13th and 14th centuries called *Kebra Nagast* ('the glory of Kings') laid down an irresistible backstory to underwrite the legitimacy of the Ethiopian emperors. A line of several hundred kings led directly back to the first Menelik, founder of the dynasty. Menelik, ten centuries before Christ, was the son of the Queen of Sheba, fruit of a stormy night she spent at the palace of King Solomon in Jerusalem. The Queen, having heard of Solomon's fame, had brought him an array of presents. The story in Ethiopia goes that Solomon put on a banquet at which he had the Queen's food specially seasoned. Afterwards he invited her to stay the night in his chambers. She agreed on condition that he swore not to force himself upon her. He promised to comply so long as she took nothing in his house. By her bedside he placed a bowl of water from which, waking thirsty in the night with the effects of all the seasoning, she drank deeply. The crafty Solomon accused her of breaking their pact, and promptly, as a historian put it, 'worked his will on her'.

Thus, proudly somehow, the great Ethiopian imperial dynasty was founded upon a rape.

In his better days, before he was forced to exit the stage in a Volkswagen, his final Highness, Haile Selasse enshrined in Article 2 of the Constitution of 1955 the following advice:

'The Imperial dignity shall remain perpetually attached to the line...[which] descends without interruption from the dynasty of Menelik I, son of the Queen of Sheba, and King Solomon of Jerusalem.'

This was partly the reason why a whole generation, like that of Sosi's mum, Ayanalem, was so surprised that the Emperor could be turfed out overnight by a group of men with no connection whatsoever to the Queen of Sheba.

One day at university, and not even particularly long after she'd started, Sosina came across her circus friends, Shannon and Alex, with whom she trained in the evenings. They were lolling around outside the campus theatre.

'What are you guys doing here?' she asked them.

'Circus auditions,' they replied.

A new circus school was opening up with a first intake of students on a twenty-week pilot scheme. If it got off the ground, it would be called the National Institute of Circus Arts: grandly, just like the national film and drama schools. Originally the brainchild of an ex–Circus Oz trapeze artist named Jane Mullett, it had latterly gathered speed, enlisting the services of an international cast of trainers, including the famous Lu Guang Rong, from Nanjing, China. (Mr Lu could balance upside down on his head with his arms and legs outstretched like a scarecrow, which might not sound impossible unless you saw him do it in the cleft of a long rope, swinging from side to side, high up in the air.)

'Can I try out, too?' Sosina asked her friends.

'You had to register weeks ago.'

She watched them disappear into the theatre for their auditions, among the line of other hopefuls. Finally, when nobody else was waiting to go in, and the last to audition had re-emerged, she took her chance and wandered out on stage in her tracksuit.

Mr Lu and the three other trainers were sitting in the empty theatre.

'Hello,' she said, smiling. Well brought up as ever.

I suppose some of the trainers scanned their lists, confirming their impression that the long afternoon of tryouts had already, perhaps mercifully, concluded.

But: 'What's your name?' said Mr Lu.

'Sosina. I heard you're doing circus auditions?'

'Yes.'

'Well, um…I can do tricks. I do the Small Companies course here but I'm a circus girl. I grew up in the circus.'

'What circus?'

She explained about Circus Ethiopia, her childhood and travelling the world. And then she warmed up and did a medley of whatever repertoire she could perform upon a bare stage: walkovers, contortions, splits, handstands…

'I can also juggle and do balances,' she said, by now gleaming with exertion. 'If I had my juggling things.'

'Okay,' said one of the trainers, noncommittal, 'hope to see you soon.'

But Mr Lu said: 'Definitely see you soon.'

And this is how Sosina negotiated to become one of the first students of the new national circus school for their twenty-week pilot course, while simultaneously completing her Small Companies Diploma.

'How about this?' she pitched to John Butler. 'While I am at NICA, I can take circus photographs and videos and interviews!'

The topic that semester at Small Companies was documentation – how to record and develop photographs and videos of performances; how to conduct interviews with those involved. (Her mother had always told Sosina: *if you don't ask, you won't get*.)

'It worked out well!' Sosina told me at the Dancing Dog café. 'I trained new circus acts,' she said, 'and at the same time took photographs and videos. I interviewed my acrobatic friends.'

Once again, I had to admire her style. I remembered that the cigarette seller liked not only bargaining but juggling, too.

11

Success and failure

If, as an asylum seeker in Australia in 1999, your appeal to the Refugee Review Tribunal was rejected, like those of Sosina and the other fourteen from the circus, you had few options left. You could appeal to the Federal Court to have your case re-examined, or hope that the Minister might grant you a visa on humanitarian grounds.

'In the Federal Court,' says Sosina dramatically, 'you were suing everybody.'

Luckily, by this stage, Sosina and her friends were being helped with their case by an experienced migration agent named Frank Fazzito. The Melbourne law firm Mallesons Stephen Jaques had offered to represent them in the Federal Court pro bono.

Sosi remembers how Frank, as she calls him, was concerned that there might have been errors or omissions in the way the cases of the fifteen asylum seekers had been handled by the Department of Immigration and the Refugee Review Tribunal.

Was it fair? Was it just? Had they followed due process in the interviewing of children under sixteen?

Had they allowed proper breaks?

Was their questioning reasonable or onerous?

Had note been taken of all the evidence?

Any big legal fight has to be built up with an accumulation of tiny blows.

Meanwhile, prompted by the allegations of abuse and mistreatment made by the fifteen young asylum seekers in Australia, Interpol and international police agencies in various countries including Ethiopia had been focusing more and more attention on Marc LaChance and his paedophile associates. Through one of the teachers at the Maribyrnong High School, Sosina and her friends heard the news that Marc LaChance had committed suicide in May, and had posted a suicide note on the front page of the Circus Ethiopia website. He had always loved boys, he admitted. He said that for this love of boys he had been destroyed, as those like him had been destroyed since Gregorian times, hounded and abused for their forbidden love. On his high horse, cornered, he blamed his imminent death on the evil children who had betrayed him in Australia. As a Buddhist (we may recall his holidays in Sri Lanka), he declared his faith that even as he died now he would soon return, as an ant or perhaps a dog.

The cases of the fifteen never reached the Federal Court. Perhaps feeling the pressure of international attention, following high-profile articles on the African-based paedophile ring in *The Guardian* and *Der Speigel,* the Immigration minister, Philip Ruddock, intervened: he would grant humanitarian visas, but only to those of the fifteen who were under eighteen. The older ones would be sent back home to Ethiopia. Frank Fazzito convened a meeting of the fifteen to discuss their response. They agreed that they couldn't accept this offer; that they would always stick together. Fazzito prepared to travel to Ethiopia to gather more evidence for the Federal Court case. But in February 2000, almost two years after the fifteen had originally sought asylum, Ruddock relented and granted humanitarian visas for the entire group.

When the news came through. Sosina was in the National Institute of Circus Arts (NICA) training space, an old wharf shed in the docklands. The circus training folk brought her a bunch of flowers with a fluffy toy kangaroo. The boss of NICA, Pam Creed, allowed Sosina to use her office phone to call Ayanalem and Tewabé in Addis Ababa. Even if Sosina hadn't confided in her parents all the ups and downs along the way – because what could they do except worry – she could share with them her triumph and relief. In only two more years now, she would be eligible for citizenship, and then at last it would be possible for her to visit them in Addis, bearing as many fluffy kangaroos as she could carry.

In the twenty weeks of the pilot program at the new circus school, they learnt a smattering of everything. Hoopdiving – although Sosi did everything she could to avoid diving through the stacked-up wooden hoops after she smashed her forehead into one, the third day in, and sat down with a migraine – tumbling, aerials, group balances, foot juggling and more.

All this circus jargon I realise I know back to front by now. Circus is a realm unto itself of distinct acts and apparatus. Some tricks are cheap sleights of hand while others are rare and precious, only acquired after countless hours of hard and often dangerous work. The secret art of circus, those adept will tell you, is to never let the audience know precisely which is which. They work at making the easy ones look difficult and the difficult ones look easy. I fell into directing circus for a few years, sideways from directing theatre. The only circus I ever directed, actually, was Circus Oz and in my case that was enough. In retrospect it's all glory and delight: fond memories of open-air Darwin parkland stretching out into a perfect tropical evening, with the crowd cheering like at a rock concert, or of the packed-out wedding cake theatre on New York's 42nd Street with, outside, New Year's Eve snow showers drifting across Times Square. But at the time it made my face break out into an exotic rash that never quite went away. Acrobats who, it is said, laugh at death, nevertheless grumble at many of the intermediate steps towards it. Some of them. Not all.

But in truth I love Circus Oz. Circus Oz embodies – very much on purpose but somehow by accident as well – many of the finer attributes of the Australian soul: a breezy openness, a rude sophistication, a faux-slapdash wit and grandeur. (Australians try very hard at appearing not to try too hard at anything we do.)

Sosina began at Circus Oz as the work experience girl, on an internship from Small Companies, after her twenty-week pilot at NICA had expired. Her role at Circus Oz was assistant stage manager and, it has to be said – as it *was* said at some length by the stage manager in her Summary Assessment to Small Companies at the end of the engagement – that in this role Sosina was an abject failure. Each performance she would scurry around, hastily and approximately setting all the backstage props and gear, then sneak away behind the audience bleachers and pop up in the aisle to watch the show. There she would absorb the performance, analyse the acts, insert herself, in her mind, into the action.

'I could do that,' she thought. 'I could be in this show.'

She couldn't really care less about what was happening backstage. Onstage. She belonged out there in the light.

She stayed an extra two weeks that season, over and above the two weeks she was meant to. At quiet times between shows, she warmed up on stage; practised her routines and tricks. She breathed in the faint sweet aroma of the departed crowd.

Starting from a low base, her value as the assistant stage manager declined steadily.

The teacher at Small Companies wanted to show Sosina the stage manager's Summary Assessment. In his office, with the door closed.

Did she have any comments?

She thought: *It always helps to know the career you don't want.*

She thought: *I have to go back to NICA so that I can get a real job. I need to be performing in a circus.*

In 2001, the pilot having been deemed successful, NICA accepted some of the erstwhile piloteers into a special second-year intake.

Sosina had observed that those successful at Circus Oz had several strings to their bow: more than one act in which they could take a leading role. She had her contortion act but needed something more. She settled on bounce-ball juggling. Some of the boys in Circus Ethiopia did it. She would be the first woman in Australia to make a bounce-ball act. Jugglers were two-a-penny but not so many could make a juggling act compelling, sexy.

At NICA therefore, in between the group acts and the basic drills, Sosina chiselled out three hours a day by herself in a quiet corner, bouncing balls.

Figuring out the timing, the trajectories, the gentle flicker of the wrists. Heights and distances. The sheen of solid marble as a platform. Spaces, gaps and moments to make eye-contact with the audience. Variety: different patterns – shotguns, twirls, cascades. With five balls set in motion in a regulated flurry, she learnt to rotate herself around them as if she was circling a firepot, her backside jaunty – remembering the dances she'd grown up with.

She practised at home, too, in the flat that she was sharing at the time. Bounce. Bounce. Bounce. On her lounge room floor. For hours at a time. She had to make friends with the Chinese people in the flat below.

Meanwhile her NICA classmates did their own thing. Everyone had his or her obsession. A wraithlike boy who'd spent years busking on the streets introduced himself as Somefish. Somefish came to NICA to learn two things only. That was all he needed. Handstands. And how to kick a goldfish lying on his foot into a bowl of water on his head. A plastic goldfish; but, nevertheless, a goldfish. After many hours and days of concentrated training, Somefish mastered first one and then the other art. The popular and the boutique. He was pleased, but that didn't make him any more amenable to attending the compulsory circus history or business classes. What did his goldfish care about history? Had he not been running his own business quite successfully, thank you, for many years? He knew how and where to place the hat, at what point to ask the audience for money, how to recognise and neutralise troublemakers. Cashflow for him was not a metaphor but something that happened on your kitchen table after work each day. When he finally quit, and the school head told him that he couldn't because he hadn't paid his fees, he went home and filled a bag with $1800 worth of five- and ten-cent coins from his under-bed repository, and placed it on her desk.

That is the best thing about circus: it attracts and (generally) accommodates all sorts. The most buttoned-up springy gymnasts. Tattooed freaks from good families who have dedicated their youth to ingesting swords and gargling fire. Ascetic vegan devotees committed to the Zen of pole-climbing or the Tao of teeter-board. Fluky kids from the bush who otherwise would be fixing cars or mowing lawns instead of hopping across a tightwire in a tutu. Divas, lost souls. Melancholics.

An Abyssinian contortionist, aficionado of the bouncing juggle; and, however briefly, a pasty white boy whose best Big Top skill was bluff and the weathering of egos:

Sosina and me.

Sosina began at Circus Oz as a bona fide performer in 2002. They'd seen her bounce-ball juggle act in a NICA show late the previous year. They knew she could do contortions. She was versatile, smart and charismatic. What's more, she was a versatile, smart and charismatic dark-skinned African-Australian ex-asylum seeker, who couldn't fail to make a cultural impression on audiences pre-tuned towards the monochromatic.

Long after I left Circus Oz, Sosina stayed – four years in all. She toured the world, but some of her richest memories are of the outback Indigenous communities where they performed, like in the Kimberley. There she developed a new understanding of Australia and the cultures of this continent.

On tour with Circus Oz around the backblocks of Australia and across the bullfighting arenas and great halls of Europe, she was given crucial lessons by John O'Hagan, then Circus Oz musical director and, to Sosi's mind, Vocabulary Man.

John took it upon himself to coach Sosi in the subtler dimensions of English pronunciation, those most idiosyncratic and difficult for foreign tongues.

Whale blubber. Whale blah-blah. *Whale blubber.* Whale blah-blah. *Whale blubber.*

Whale blubber.

Comfortable. Com-fort-ay-bull. *Comf-t'ble.* Com-fort-ay-bull. *Comf-t'ble.*

Comf-t'ble.

Just as important as mastering these phonetic codes was mastering the distinctive Australian sense of humour. Dry as a Methodist wedding. Early in her time at Circus Oz it was well known that half an hour could elapse between the telling of a joke and Sosina laughing at that joke. On buses and planes, in hotel rooms and restaurants, she worked on improving joke-to-laugh times and eliminating whale blah-blah, with the concentration of the long-distance bounce-ball juggler and the wiles of the contortionist.

On the way home to Australia from a Circus Oz tour in Europe, Sosi stopped off to visit her brother Abraham in Cairo. Abraham was two years older than Sosina, and the sibling she felt closest to. Abraham had fled to Egypt from Ethiopia because of fears he held for his safety in the volatile political environment. By this time, despite his UN-recognised status as a refugee, Sosina's requests to bring him to Australia had been refused twice by the Australian Immigration Department. No grounds given. Caught in limbo, he was starting to lose hope.

This is the last time she would ever see him.

'Cairo,' says Sosi, 'was very hot.'

'You see all of these hopeful Ethiopians there. You look at them and it's like they haven't started their life yet. They are just waiting, for survival. Most of the women have jobs cleaning people's houses. But there aren't many jobs for the guys. Abraham was going to school.

'They are very supportive of each other, like Ethiopians are in any of these situations, like in Kenya. But in Cairo, Christians are in a minority so that makes the Ethiopian Christians like Abraham stick together more. They go to church together.'

'I got in trouble,' she says, 'because I was showing my skin. Abraham told me they would expect me to be fully covered. But it was hot! I wore a Circus Oz T-shirt, not like a halter-neck or anything. But any little piece of left-over skin that's showing, the men will stare at. On your neck or your arm, it's like they are drawn to that tiny piece of skin. It's bizarre!' She laughs.

'All these men are calling out: *I can be your husband! I can be your husband!* Abraham said: *It's because you are showing that skin.* It was like they went mad because they never saw any.

'I treated him: we did tourist things. We went on this boat on the Nile. As an Ethiopian, being on the Nile is a weird feeling, because – because Ethiopia is not allowed to use the Nile! Because it takes all the soil, all the minerals out of the country; that's what Egypt is living on. And the Ethiopian people are starved!' She laughs again, this time at her own blunt version of the facts.

'Now the Ethiopian government has decided to build a dam on the Blue Nile so they can produce electricity, but it's a big fight.

All the land along the Nile was irrigated and producing so much, with the irrigation. It all looked so beautiful, and it made me think of how dry it was back in Ethiopia. It's always been a tension. But I think it's a big river and they should all be able to share it. All of these things I'm thinking when we're on the Nile – how expensive it is to buy fresh fruit in Ethiopia and how cheap it is in Cairo.

'Then we went to the pyramids. Abraham and I both rode on camels. They are so cruisey the way they walk, just like a big sofa. They make you move so slow; I could easily go to sleep on one, I reckon.

'The tour guides said: *You're not allowed to climb those pyramids.* Because we wanted to get a photo taken. So I said to Abraham: *What about if we give them a little bit of money? Will they allow us to pass? Does that work here?* He said: *Yeah, of course, give it a shot.*

'I handed them money; they didn't even look at it. They said: *Quick, quick, quick, go and get your photo taken.*'

She chuckles briefly at the memory: 'I have those photos somewhere.'

At the pinnacle of Sosina's career with Circus Oz, they performed a season at the Sydney Opera House – the first ever by the company. Sosi felt proud to be part of this historic moment. The company posed in costume for photographs backstage, before the wall of windows that looks out to the great arch and towers of the Harbour Bridge. Sosi can be seen beaming in their midst.

But as she came offstage one night, after the long applause, there was a message on her mobile. She pressed her caked-on face to the phone.

It was from her brother's friend in Cairo. Abraham had taken an overdose of pills. The next time could be fatal.

'Everybody thinks that young men are strong; that's the problem. Australia or Canada or England will usually think to take women or elders first, because they think young men in their thirties are the strongest and they can handle it; they won't suffer depression. But I think everyone deserves a place, regardless of their age or sex. He had in the end three rejections, and a long, long process.

'I remember thinking: *You must be kidding me, he's got a UN card as a refugee in Egypt, I'm his immediate family, and still you rejected me to bring him here.* So what would you do the next round? You have to adjust your application to try to make yourself be believed; and still that didn't work, until he died.

'He was taking a lot of painkillers, for migraines and stress. His friend was really worried about him taking so many pills. That's why he rang me.

'A few times I talked to Abraham on the phone and could put the puzzle together. It was really horrible thinking, *Here I am part of history, the first time Circus Oz is performing in the Opera House, and I cannot even help my brother; he is probably dying, in very, very deep problems.*

'I was worried he might die of an overdose without even meaning to. He didn't drink or smoke, he was a very clean person. But he had so much stress and chronic migraines.

'He was refused three times, and every time he was refused the process took longer. And it was very hard to find someone in the Immigration Department to talk to about his case.

'I just kept saying to him, *You have to wait. You have to wait. You have to wait and see.*

'What else could I tell him?'

At around about this time, Sosina was made Young Victorian of the Year and nominated for the Australia Day Awards. They put her on a poster. At the top left it says: *Australia Day – Celebrate What's Great.* At the bottom right it says: *Department of Immigration and Multicultural Affairs.* It's a stunning photo of her from side-on, almost a silhouette. She is wearing her sexy, skin-tight black latex allover costume from Circus Oz and balancing on her forearms with her legs arched all the way back and around, to almost touch her fingers. She looks resolutely out in front of her. Superimposed across her body are her own words, handwritten: *As a refugee, now Australian citizen, I have found a new home with Australia and its people, whose tolerance I value, whose diversity I respect, and in whose hearts I hope will remain enough human kindness for all.*

Australia, Australia, floating so far away out in the ocean, all by itself. This will be the first place that will sink.

12

The price of living

Sosi's life has welled up in catastrophe. Her dad: his cancer.

Generations in the West all know the story of the 'Third World'; we live with it tucked away in the peripheral vision of our conscience. In the First World, if I want hot water, I walk to the tap and turn it on. If I am upstairs in the new extension of our inner-city house I have to wait at least a minute for the water to turn hot. I watch as all the other water not hot enough for my taste smashes down the drain. I consider what a waste it is, and that I possibly should be trying to catch it somehow, to divert it to a more productive fate (perhaps pour it on the garden). But then the new water starts to warm my finger and I forget about the earlier water I was a moment ago so concerned with. I push down the plug and start to make a pond in the ceramic basin to dunk the razor in. This trial of waiting at least a minute for the water to turn hot in the upstairs bathroom, with its attendant vaguely flowing guilt, is the limit of my difficulty with hot water. But I know – everyone knows, we've seen it on TV – that in Somalia, or why not say Ethiopia, in the countryside, one might have to walk kilometres to fill up a plastic container with water close enough to fresh, and that heating it will be a whole other matter, and that it could be much worse if a drought comes or a war. Everyone knows all this. *That is how the world is*, we might think, or: *Hey, I give to Oxfam direct-debit once a month.* But the point is: Sosi's dad. If he were my dad, assuming I had a dad, and he had cancer – well, for a start, my brother would know the absolute best way to get the best treatment from the finest medical specialists, because he's a professor at the hospital. We would make sure our imaginary dad saw the right person straightaway; we would ask all the right questions; we would assess all the options. Like middle-class, well-educated superheroes, we would leap into action without even changing our Clark Kent clothes. And all of this would have happened months or years ago, at the first early warning we detected.

For Sosi, as an Ethiopian–Australian, nothing is so simple. For six months she has negotiated with doctors. She has negotiated with hospitals. She has negotiated with Immigration. She has tried to convince Immigration she's not lying, he's really sick, he's not going to want to stay on in Australia, it's not all an elaborate ruse. There are paperwork and procedures enough to bamboozle and frustrate any of us. The implacable system, thinking of itself as neutral, fair. For those of us born on the developed-world side of the invisible fence that zigzags the globe, these types of everyday problems are invisible, too.

Sosi's first application for a temporary medical visa for her father was rejected. No reasons given (but you would have to think: they didn't believe her). She reapplied, supplying further information and with a letter of support from Circus Oz. The second application was rejected. No reasons given. She enlisted help to talk directly with Australian consular officials in Kenya, from where Ethiopian visa applications are processed. Finally, miraculously, the third application was accepted (no reasons given).

Tewabé is on a plane. Sosi has bought a ticket for him to leave Ethiopia for only the second time in his life (after years ago visiting Germany with the St George Brewery engineers). He leaves behind Ayanalem, still tethered to her oxygen bottle and commanding from her bed – the bridge of her ship, as it were – the hotel, restaurant and café they have built around their home in Addis Ababa; Ayanalem praying all the more now, and with such good reason, to the handsome, colourful Jesus on her wall.

The evening Tewabé arrives in Melbourne Sosina is performing with the *Burlesque Hour* in a country town. She drives home to discover him still up at 2 am, chatting at the kitchen table with Mel and Sosi's sister, Meski. Tewabé greets his beloved daughter just like any father would, grumbling: 'Why do you have to work so late? Until 2 am?'

The specialist orders the standard battery of tests. Tewabé waits at the house in St Albans for the first report to come.

But after a week or so Sosina notices how pale he looks. 'Dad,' she says, 'you don't look well.'

'I'm fine,' he says. 'Let's wait for the report.'

'But, Dad, you've stopped eating, you've stopped moving around, and you can't even sit down; I've been watching.'

'I'm not too bad,' he insists. 'But the wound on my backside hurts: maybe that's infected.'

'I'm taking you to the doctor now,' she says.

They go to a GP they have never visited before. He briefly examines Tewabé's buttocks and anus in his consulting room. 'Oh my God!' he says, clearly shocked.

'I think this is anal cancer,' he looks at Sosina, 'and he will die.'

Tewabé doesn't understand English. Every conversation like this, Sosina forces herself to smile so that he won't suspect the worst.

'I think it is anal cancer mixed up with a large infection,' says the GP.

'Okay,' says Sosina, smiling.

'It's likely he will die.'

'Okay,' she makes herself nod. She's sitting, smiling on the chair, while her father lies beside her.

'Who is paying for this?' Asks the doctor.

'I'm paying,' she says.

'I think you're wasting your money; he's going to die regardless. I don't know how much time he's got.'

She puts this to one side.

'Can you do something for his pain?'

'I'm not going to touch him. You have to take him to Emergency.'

She smiles again and thanks him.

They get back in the car.

'That GP wasn't an expert in this area so we have to take you to the hospital,' she tells him calmly.

Then she is aware of Tewabé saying this and that as they drive along but, deafened by her fears, she doesn't hear a word.

After queuing at Emergency, he is admitted to the hospital. Within a couple of hours the specialist comes by.

He greets Tewabé. Then he turns to Sosina and says, 'Would you like to talk here or outside?'

'It's okay, we can talk here; he doesn't speak English,' she replies.

'Well, we think he's got bowel cancer and that's what's caused the infection in his buttock.'

'Okay,' she says calmly, like she had done with the doctor.

'We need to operate immediately.'

And then are a host of questions to fill out on a form so as to indemnify the doctors and the hospital.

'Has he ever had a heart attack?'

'Dad, have you ever had a heart attack?'

'Oh, no,' says Tewabé, 'I've never had anything like that.'

(Sosina adds here in parentheses: 'That story changed later on, I tell you!')

'No, no,' he says, to all the questions.

'Okay, if you can sign here on his behalf...?'

As soon as she has signed the form, they wheel him away to surgery. It takes six hours. When the surgeon re-emerges, he says: 'I've never before in my career seen a tumour that large in the bowel. It must've been growing there for years.'

Tewabé is placed in an induced coma to recover from the surgery.

After a week has gone by they ask Sosina: 'Shall we wake your father up now?'

'Yes,' she says. 'Please do.'

As he comes out of the coma he begins hallucinating. He says to Sosi, 'Come! Come! Come! Mimi!' He says it very quietly, whispering in Amharic.

She says, 'You don't have to whisper, Dad; we are in Australia, none of these people speak Amharic.'

He disagrees, suspicious, whispering: 'These people speak four languages!' He says: 'I want you to record me. I want you to record what I have to say, because I am going to die in two hours, and I need you to record what I have to tell you.'

She grabs her phone to record him with, and he starts telling her about the people who had died mysteriously in the Haile Selasse days, the people who had died likewise in the days of the Derg government of Mengistu, and all the other people who had died. When he is finished, he says: 'Now, everything you have recorded, you have to write down.'

'Write down?'

'Take it to those ladies who are downstairs with the type-writers' – because, says Sosi, in the hospital in Addis back in the old days (Haile Selasse time?), there were indeed ladies downstairs with typewriters – 'take it to those ladies,' he says, 'Bring it back to me, and I'll sign it for you.'

The nurses tell Sosi that it is common in intensive care for the drugs to make the patients hallucinate like this. But Tewabé tells her that in fact the nurses are the very ones who want to kill him. Particularly the male nurse with the big needle in his hand. He is going to kill him now, with that needle.

Sosi tells me: 'Sometimes I just cracked up laughing.'

Three or four days later, Sosina wakes up at home at 5 am knowing something isn't right. She calls Tewabé in the hospital.

'My heart is beating a lot,' he says.

'Do you have a chest pain?'

'I have a massive chest pain.'

Panic-stricken, Sosina drives straight to the Western Hospital in her pyjamas. She runs inside and finds a doctor.

'He has a chest pain!' she says.

'How do you know?' asks the doctor.

'He told me!'

The doctor sweeps into action, ordering a scan straightaway. Looking at the results of the scan, he says the bad news is that Tewabé has had a moderate heart attack. Not only that but he must have had two previous heart attacks in Ethiopia. The scars are visible.

I don't know what the good news was.

Next, the specialist comes back with a report about the cancer. It is in Tewabé's lymph glands. Incurable. Six months of chemotherapy would slow it down, might give him two or five or ten years. 'You can't see the cancer on an X-ray,' says the specialist, 'It isn't in his liver or his lungs. In the glands it is hidden, and you never know where it will emerge. It's like chasing a horse,' he tells her. She repeats the phrase: *like chasing a horse.*

Although the surgeon is pro bono, the hospital is not. For a foreign national it costs $2400 per day in intensive care plus costs, and then $700 per day in a normal ward, plus costs. At least she doesn't have to pay upfront before they will treat him, as might happen in other countries. But the hospital's finance committee is concerned. Sosi needs to sign a letter and she needs to sign it here and now in this room, not after the weekend, not on Monday. Somehow, sometime, with the details yet to be established, she takes responsibility for the bill up till now, doesn't she? This is only the bill to date: $37,000. On behalf of her dad she has racked that up in about a fortnight. She rings Mel at work. He says, 'You can't argue with them; you can't put them offside. You have to work with them.'

She is told Tewabé will need to be in hospital for two months.

'That's another $30,000,' I tell her helpfully.

'I think it will be a hundred thousand in the end,' she says. 'I cannot think,' she says. 'It's all too much to think about,' she says. 'I just think about each day.'

The following Sunday she organises a benefit night to raise money.

Circus Oz have lent her their Spiegeltent for the evening for no charge. Sosi has called and Facebooked all of her circus and theatre friends for help: someone will run the bar, others will do the lights, the sound, set up a website for donations, sell tickets at the door, stage manage the performance, donate paintings for the auction, sell raffle tickets, MC the night, buy finger food...then there are the performers: performance art, circus, contemporary dance, traditional Ethiopian dance, more circus (always circus).

On the night, Sosi's sister Meski sets up a coffee ceremony inside the entrance to the Spiegeltent, coffee bubbling in a pot on a little coal burner set on grass mats. Incense threads the air around two plump bowls of popcorn. Sosi's daughter Raeey, now two years old, dressed up in bows and a party dress, hugs the corner of the bar. A swag of people from the Ethiopian community settle in to the tables nearest the stage. They mostly drink Coke; not good news for profits on the bar.

Ex–Circus Oz performer Anni Davey plays the compere, in a long black dress and splendid chunky heels. She warms the room up with her patter, bridging the cultural divide between the more weird of the circus and performance folks and the Ethiopian families with small children. Later she plucks out $50 bills from her splendid bosom to lead the bidding in the auction. The Ethiopians in the audience bid first for all the items. It is hard to beat them. One man buys an Ethiopian Cross and donates it right back again so that it can be bid for and bought again.

Moira Finucane, a Melbourne cabaret performer, performs a lascivious meat pie–eating scene dressed as a nurse all in white, saturated with irony and soon smeared with tomato sauce. An acrobat called Moses enters in misshapen white face and large green wooden clogs, his body bare from the waist up; he hauls himself up on a rope, climbing toe by toe, wrapping and knotting the rope around him; he spins, drops, the rope yanks against his kidneys. Off he comes and climbs again.

Sosi herself works overtime. First she performs her latest bounce-ball juggle act, standing on a wooden chair in her racy burlesque kit. She's tired and misses tricks she wouldn't normally. Not that it matters. She has enough tricks to spare a few gone wrong. Later she returns with a hula-hoop routine. Then she leads two compatriots in a medley of Ethiopian regional dances, each a minute or two of high energy and colour, interspersed with rapid costume changes.

At some point in the evening Sosi makes a speech, explaining what we're here for. Even though I think I know it all already, I understand some things anew. 'We didn't want to take a risk like with my mother,' she says. 'My mother went into hospital in Addis Ababa eleven years ago for a simple operation to have gallstones removed. They made mistakes with the operation and she's been on oxygen ever since.'

'This is our culture,' says Sosi, holding the microphone like the professional she is. 'In Ethiopia we all come together to support our families.'

Tewabé comes out of hospital around the time the bill hits $70,000. The day I drive out to visit them at St Albans, the mid-morning December sun is already bleaching hot.

The grass is knee-high in the garden, but for where the car has flattened it. The backyard wavers in the breeze, a rectangle of neglect between the wooden fences. 'Yeah, the mower broke,' says Sosi philosophically. This is the least important misfortune that has befallen them.

She's met me at the door in her pyjamas. 'Hi, Dave.' A little kiss on the cheek, but tiredness emanates from the house like a draught. Raeey rushes past Sosi's legs into the lounge room. Tewabé is lying on the couch, a white cotton blanket draped around him in the Ethiopian style. He lifts himself up to welcome me and shake my hand. He looks older and thinner than he had done eighteen months previously in Addis in his own lounge room, watching his beloved Manchester United rather than the wash of cartoons left behind here by his granddaughter. Older and thinner, but not impossibly so. Better than he looked in the photo from the hospital, lain out beneath the weight of medical technology.

The curtains are closed, perhaps against the heat or perhaps because they just *are* closed, the same as the grass just *has* grown, and the television just *is* on, blaring animations. I can't believe he actually likes this stuff; but perhaps, again, he uses it as a colourful veil over his immediate surroundings, in front of which he can project, with the clarity the painkillers afford, certain scenes that come effortlessly to mind: visions of Addis, his favourite patio there, the waterpipe that needs fixing, the St George beer factory and the countryside of his childhood, faces, the faces of his many friends and relations, and always Ayanalem who is needing him.

He shakes my hand and we greet each other warmly. I give him the panforte I have bought from the Mediterranean Supermarket on Sosi's recommendation, feeling pleased to be able to come with a gift he might enjoy. I suppose those dry Italian cakes are another of Mussolini's legacies back home in Addis. We exchange a few words of small talk, or at least I proffer a few authentically felt if anodyne fragments of conversation, the sort of thing one learns to do if well brought up in my culture, the sort of thing that generally leads to something else like a cup of tea or an invitation to sit down, and even possibly to a more meaningful conversation in good time. Tewabé smiles and nods and makes appropriate nonspecific utterances in reply, for he is well brought up, too, and an expert at making a good show of participating in dialogues in a language more or less completely foreign. Tewabé would be a great poker player and I can never tell (it was the same in Addis) when my meagre chatty gambits have slipped past the point where he has any idea what I am talking about. By contrast, as soon as he turns to talk to Sosi in Amharic, he is confident from the first word that I am lost.

Sosi and I take Raeey to childcare in Sosi's bomby car. 'I'm going to drive it till it stops; the mechanic said it's not worth fixing,' she tells me. As soon as the engine switches on, Raeey, trussed up on her foam seat in the back, squeals, 'I wanna game! Game! Game!'

'Usually I let her play with my phone,' sighs Sosi. Evidently Raeey's out of luck this time. She gives up – or forgets about it – before the corner of the street, and looks out of the window at the cars and trucks and houses and scraggly urban fields of western Melbourne, as Sosi sweeps the car this way and that down a succession of backstreets and side ways that you have the feeling only she might know about – she and her Ethiopian taxi-driving friends – until we turn up three suburbs later at the childcare centre. Which is vast but in a good way: an old house surrounded on all sides by outdoor carpet and a battalion of plastic vehicles, with further houses out the back and further houses beyond them, under the trees, by the sandpits, where the small inhabitants can be found, busy in their games, mid-sentence, looking at us like we're aliens.

The hooks where the children hang their backpacks, the low-slung scale of things, the plywood drawers and boxes of toys polished by so many tiny hands; it reminds me of when I took my children to the creche on Glenlyon Road in Brunswick, signed them in and left them there, already absorbed with their friends, not noticing me leave. Raeey runs off in just the same way, greeted by the carer as if she is a latecomer at a party whom everyone's been waiting for.

'I like to get her in before eleven,' says Sosi, who, being a performer, is not a morning person. This way she can be sure Raeey gets to eat lunch at creche: they provide good, healthy food.

I notice the diversity in the creche crowd 'out here' – both the kids and carers look like they might have been gathered together as a representative cross-section of all the new immigrant communities of Melbourne: Pacific, Asian, African, Middle-Eastern. Back in inner-city 'multicultural' Brunswick, where I live, which is much more multicultural than that great swathe of affluence stretching east and south of the city, we are nonetheless somewhat kidding ourselves, I conclude.

Sosi wraps the car around all the same corners, heading home again, and the warm north wind slices in through the window.

'Every week they've been sending six or seven different bills,' she says. 'I don't believe it! You get different ones for the pharmacy, for the ward, for everything. I rang the pharmacy and I said to them, *Don't send me this bill separate from the other ones. You're all in the one hospital; surely you can send me one bill for everything, each time?*'

When she finds out the total cost until now, not including the six months of chemotherapy Tewabé might need, she will make the hospital an offer. *Flat price*, she will say, *Take it or leave it. If you don't take it you'll get nothing because I don't have any more money.* This is the type of negotiation that would never occur to me, non-cigarette seller that I am.

'Well,' she says, 'you know they charge a lot for things – you have to buy every single thing he needs from the hospital; even cotton buds. You can't pay for your own: you can't buy a normal cotton bud for five cents; theirs will cost you forty cents.

'How do you know what they charge for cotton buds?'

'Everything is itemised on the bill,' she says.

Meski has prepared lunch for all of us. My eyes light up now at the sight of the *injera* and the *wat*. We drink Ethiopian black coffee, admiring the aroma of the freshly roasted beans.

Tewabé has retired to the carport, where he likes to lie on a mattress on these hot days, preferring the open air to the boxy house. 'He doesn't eat,' says Sosi. All the time she is telling him he needs to eat.

'I don't feel hungry,' he tells her, but she says: 'You have to get strong; you have to eat!' He is an elder and the head of the family and it doesn't come naturally to follow the orders of his daughter.

'You need to eat to get strong so that you can go home and look after our mother,' says Sosina, laying out her trump. He chews a few things.

He doesn't like to take the painkillers either – he believes that in the long run that sort of thing is not good for you – but if he stops taking them the pain is unbearable.

When I go out to say goodbye he is standing in the shade, moving gently from leg to leg, no doubt to ease the pressures on his muscles, joints and organs. He has wrapped his cotton blanket across both shoulders so that he looks, to my eyes, like a picture from a *National Geographic* magazine – which I know is wrong to say but is typical of the stuff I find deposited in my mind – an undoubtedly proud and, yes, noble, Ethiopian elder, a man of the countryside who in the picture would be standing in late-afternoon light upon an immense plateau outside the village of his grandmother with rocky crags behind (beside a headline like 'An ancient civilisation on the edge'), rather than on the four squares of shade made by the concrete floor beneath the crinkled carport in front of the garage doors at his daughter's house in a country floating in the middle of an ocean. It might be the effect of the painkillers or the disease but he seems massively self-contained; not resigned but definitely, one would say, stoic. Most of all, distant. Every part of him except his body is already back home in Ethiopia. It is as if he is focusing his mind on transporting the rest of himself there, atom by atom, working on the formula for doing so just as he would have solved any other engineering challenge with the Germans at the St George brewery.

13

The right time and the wrong time

One day while Tewabé is still in the hospital, no longer in intensive care but on the ward, the doctors say to Sosina: 'We need to talk to your father and we don't want you to translate for him this time. There are things he needs to know about his condition.' The doctors suspect, as is absolutely true, that Sosi doesn't always translate word for word. She sees her job as translating not only between two languages but two cultures. And in her culture one shelters loved ones from the truth if one feels that is what is best for them. What good would it do him to know his lung had collapsed? It wouldn't change anything for the better; it might only make him lose hope that he would return home soon. She told him he had a heart attack because he needed to know so that he could look out for early danger signs next time around. But she hadn't told him his chance of surviving was fifty-fifty – how would that help? Besides, the more he knew, the more he was likely to tell Ayanalem (he wouldn't be able to stop himself, says Sosi), and that was the greatest danger of all: the terrible worry it would cause her, when just one more thing on top of everything else she lived with – the blood pressure, the diabetes, the asthma, the weak lungs and heart – might tip her over, beyond saving.

Can you imagine how exhausting it must be for Sosina to juggle all these secrets day and night? Her brother and her sister back in Addis, her brother in Toronto, even her sister living here in the very same house; none of them know anything more than the faintest edge of what's been happening these last six and twelve months. Singlehandedly she is holding back the piled-up wreck of truths from her entire extended family. Somehow it has befallen her, or she has taken on the role, having skipped off on the train that night from Sydney to a new life as a First World citizen, to be responsible for the welfare of them all. Life and death.

'I am the only one who knows everything,' she says. 'About my mum's illnesses, my dad's conditions, what the doctors are thinking, the finances, the fundraising, the family arrangements, childcare...It isn't easy not to tell my dad but to tell him would be harder for him. I'm constantly thinking: *Should I tell him this? No. Should I tell him that? No. Should I tell my mum that? Definitely not. That might kill her.* Every day there is something new. I think: *Well, I can tell that to Mel, because Mel knows everything. Meski? Yes, she should know about that too because she'll figure it out for herself in a few days and then I'll be in trouble so I should tell her. Mum? No. My dad? No. All the extended family, my friends? No.* Because one of them might let it slip. It's just a game you keep playing to protect everyone. You don't want to play this game but you don't have any choice. People in the West get angry if they're not told things. But in Ethiopia, if people find out later, they understand why it was you didn't tell them. They would do the same. So I keep all of this information. I am like a mad woman.'

'We need to talk to Mr Wogayehu directly,' say the doctors.

'Don't worry; I can translate everything,' she says, but they have obviously had some discussions of their own, behind closed doors, as it were, and determined a course of action that involves bringing in an official translator. Sosi is concerned: if they are going to tell him his condition with the cancer cannot be cured, that he has not many months left, this will upset him so badly, worrying about no longer being able to take care of his wife, that he might have another heart attack then and there. The situation seems to be veering out of her control. But when the translator arrives Sosi sees that it is a woman she knows well from the Ethiopian community, and she winks at her. The doctors tell Tewabé his prognosis as clearly and plainly as they can. 'Your cancer has spread into the glands,' they say. 'It may have gone too far for treatment by chemotherapy to be of benefit.' Et cetera, et cetera. The woman translates in a fully professional manner, choosing the best words for the situation, and everyone is satisfied. She doesn't have to meet Sosina's gaze.

As it happens, for a long while each time I showed Sosi sections of this manuscript I left bits out. It might be best to show her those parts later, I told myself. They might make her worry that I am taking the book in the wrong direction, whatever direction that might be. I just cut them out, for the time being, without mentioning them. In my case, no doubt, I wasn't thinking of her best interests so much as my own, but on the other hand perhaps I was thinking, too: *What good will come of showing her those bits now? It might only upset her in some way. I'll show them to her later, when the time is right…*I know, it's hardly life and death, in this instance; it's only a writer's connivances, but I suppose my bigger point is that all day long we find ourselves negotiating stories, counting out the size and shape of those we will or won't tell as if upon old-fashioned weighing scales, which threaten to tip over on one side into pain and upset if the stories pile up too high or else crash back the other way with silence floating in the air.

Another phone call. Sosi, flatter than ever…'Hi, Dave.' Her voice parched as if she's been walking all day under a hot sun.

'How are you, Sos?'

'Oh…it's not good news.' Saying it as lightly as she can.

'I had to take him back into hospital yesterday, after midnight. He'd been having pain with his urine and he started pissing blood, and then it started clotting so it was blocked.

'In the hospital they told me: *The cancer has invaded the bottom of his bladder.* They can't remove his bladder – he wouldn't survive the surgery. *He's really dying now,* they said. *You should take him home. He might have weeks or months. There's a small window if you want to take him home to Ethiopia.*'

She spoke to Mel. He agreed: she must take Tewabé home to Addis as soon as possible, as soon as he is well enough to fly. He needs to go home to see his family. She will take him home herself and stay there with Raeey for however long she needs to.

Once again she won't tell Tewabé the prognosis, and she won't tell any of her family back in Addis – not over the phone, not from this distance. She doesn't want them greeting him with tears when he arrives. What good would that do? She wants her mother and her father to be happy when they are reunited, for being happy will surely give their health a boost. At the very least it will give them some good moments together.

She has told Meski because Meski will need to travel back with Sosina, Raeey and Tewabé, because now is the time that the family should be all together. For the same reason, she needed to tell her brother Yonatan in Toronto. He will defer his university course for four months to go home, too. She will pay, somehow.

Sosi accepts that she has exhausted every Western treatment option. She says: 'He needs to drink Holy Water now. He needs to go to church and drink Holy Water. It can cure people, you know. If they believe in it. My mother drinks Holy Water every day.

That's probably why she has survived this long, with everything she has wrong with her; she drinks Holy Water from the church. There is a beggar who brings her Holy Water often. When she washes her head in Holy Water, it calms her down.

'My mum, she's sick every single night, between midnight and six in the morning, but when the sun comes up she thanks God that she has lived to see another day and she is happy. My dad, he's like an opposite. He always said, *My God, if you are there, why did you do this to my wife? Why did you make her suffer like this?*'

One night in the hospital, Tewabé has a vision. He believes that he is back in Lalibela, in the mountains so many days north of Addis, where the ancient churches have been hewn from solid rock dug out beneath the ground. This is the place he used to journey to with friends each year, at the time of the annual ritual ceremonies.

He is chanting softly. He says to Sosina, 'Can you see the priest? It's Lalibela. Lalibela.'

Sosi looks around but all she can see is the white walls of the hospital ward and the machines beep-beeping everywhere.

'Should I come?' I ask. 'To Ethiopia? Would this be a good time for me to come? I don't want to intrude upon your family...'

'Yes, I think it is a good time,' she says, 'You should come in February, a few weeks from now. The whole family will be there. I think it is a good time, an important time for you to see.'

She asks me if I have a video camera. I wonder what she might be thinking of us filming.

When Sosi takes Tewabé back to Ethiopia, she will have to transport all of his medical supplies with her, since nothing will be easily available. All of them: the colostomy bags, the expensive heavy duty painkillers and the gauzes and bandages for the scars from the plastic surgery on his buttocks that still need to be cleaned and dressed each day (Sosi and Meski have taught themselves how to do this since there will be no nurses to pay home-visits in Addis Ababa).

'You know, Dave,' she says to me in passing, 'I have met a lot of amazing people. I met this woman doctor in the outpatients. I was telling her my story and she just cried and cried. She wanted to help me; she talked to her friends in palliative care. They were not supposed to help my dad because he was international but they have started coming around to visit him in the hospital bed. They are so nice. They are giving him painkillers, whatever he needs. And I became friends with the woman in charge of the colostomy bags. When she heard about how much I have to pay for everything she sent around an email to all of her colleagues, all of the colostomy people in the different hospitals, asking them if they could send her any spare bags for me to take home to Ethiopia. They sent altogether three whole boxes – a year's supply! People are so generous when you ask for things. And now, when I am so desperate, I will ask anybody. No harm in asking. If they say no, that's okay; I will just ask. It is like when I used to jump over the ticket barriers to get on the train in those days when I had no money. I feel just like that again now. I have nothing to lose! I have nothing already! I am so far in debt!'

Finally, she says: 'You know, they have even told me how my father will die. The oncologist told me that if the cancer was in the liver it would be a very painful death, but in my father's case it is in the bladder and what will happen is that it will move up slowly into the kidney, and then he will become more and more tired and sleepy and pass away in his sleep, with no pain.'

'Well – I suppose that at least is something,' I offer.

'Yes,' she agrees. 'But every time now that he is tired and wants to sleep I worry…

Sosi ran one final battle for Tewabé, but time, as ever this past year, was against her. The hospital had said that there was a small window in which he would be well enough to fly home. Once he came out of hospital again for the last time, they gave her the medical certificate the airlines needed. In the comments box they wrote: *Patient wants to be able to go home to die with his family.* The first airline freaked out. They said it would cost $40,000 upfront to fly him business class because he would need two nurses on board for constant medical attention. Sosi told the airline that she didn't have $40,000 upfront (which was true, of course) but tried to bargain the price down. She was sure she could make it much cheaper for the airline because she would take care of getting him to and from each airport, and she and Meski could even do the nursing because they had been trained up by the nurses at the hospital to administer all of the medication he required; because after all they would be doing everything for him after he landed in Ethiopia. The story gets a little confusing around here, but it seems someone at the airline freaked out even more and they changed their mind and said they wouldn't take him at all under any circumstances, and insisted on refunding the return ticket he already had. Sosi thought the problem might lie with the comment in the comment box from the hospital – *home to die* – which they had only made in trying to be helpful, but which seemed to be having the opposite effect, and she thought that if it was possible to change that comment in the comment box…So she drove one more time back to the hospital, first thing in the morning, and asked them to issue a new certificate with a different comment, or no comment at all, since the comment box was optional and no comment might be more helpful than the one she had; and the people at the hospital were more than happy to help out, and she took the new form and sent it straightaway to two other airlines that, between them, flew the two legs of another route to Addis Ababa.

But neither of these two airlines would consider flying him.

For a week or so he stayed at home at Sosi's house and they cared for him there. He was eating and drinking, but sleepy, sleepier each day.

Sosina prayed for a miracle. She stayed up all night searching on the Internet to learn what to expect if you were watching someone die in front of you. One day she noticed that Tewabé's feet were turning blue.

Sosi's youngest brother, Yonatan, lives alone in Toronto, Canada. He is a marathon runner; he grew up running marathons through the quiet predawn streets of Addis. For training, he and his friends used to run on trails through the forests of Entoto above the city, where the altitude was even higher and you might come face to face with a hyena, as Yonatan did one day. (Handy tip: he stared it down, because if you throw a rock at a hyena it will know that you don't have any stronger weapons and it will no longer be afraid of you.)

Sosi had tried to help Yonatan emigrate from Ethiopia to Australia. She had tried to persuade the Australian Institute of Sport to sponsor him as an elite athlete. They thought about it, so she says, but he wasn't World Top Ten.

Yonatan travelled to Canada for a race in 2006 and sought asylum there. Within six months he was accepted. He was given assistance to finish high school and won a scholarship to enrol in a university degree in sports management. But it was too cold in Toronto to train all year round to be a champion marathon runner, so he had to put aside that dream.

He had been planning to come to Australia in the northern summer to see his dad recuperate, if Sosi could afford the airfare. But now she called him to say he must come straight away. Tewabé would not survive long. Yonatan deferred from his studies, organised his rent and bills, closed up his flat and a week later landed in Melbourne.

Tewabé said – because the painkillers were so strong that he was often seeing things and he hadn't laid eyes on his youngest son for six years – 'Is that really you?'

'Yes, it's me,' said Yonatan. 'I have flown here thirty-seven hours to see you. How do you think I look? Do you think I've changed?'

In the last days, Tewabé went back to hospital. Sosina didn't have the wherewithal to care for him at home, with a two-year-old on her hands. Sosi, Meski and Yonatan took turns to sit at Tewabé's bedside in the hospital.

Two days before he died Sosina had a big fight with the nurse. The nurse said: 'This will be the last drip we will give him.'

Sosina asked her: 'Why is that? He's not dead yet!'

'Well,' the nurse said, 'he is dying anyway and it will create too much fluid around his lung so I'm not going to give him any more.'

Sosina was furious. She said to the nurse: 'I'm paying $760 a day for this bed and I have a right to ask for a drip for my father!'

'I guess,' she reflects to me now that time has passed, 'I wasn't accepting that he was dying. But also, he was still conscious! I felt terrible that he might be feeling thirsty. Or hungry.'

The nurse said: 'The doctor ordered it.'

Sosi said: 'Call the doctor.'

The doctor came.

Sosi said: 'I want a drip for my father. You can make it slower if you like, but I want a drip for him!'

'They were trying to make him die more quickly but I didn't want that. I wanted him to die when he would die,' she explains to me.

The next day, another nurse said, 'This will be his last drip. The doctor ordered this.'

Sosi said: 'Call the doctor.'

Another doctor came. He said, 'He's dying anyway.'

Sosi said, 'I don't care if he's dying.'

So they gave him another drip.

'I had a feeling,' she says now, 'that it was the last day. You know, because he looked much healthier that day. His eyes were wide.'

Sosi asked the nurse if Meski and she could wash him. They took their time; they sponged him in the bed and talked to him. 'I was so scared to say anything, that this could be the day. I was so scared that it would come out of my mouth and he would just die, like that, there and then. So I left,' she explains to me.

They came home, leaving Yonatan behind with him.

Meski went to bed; Sosi sat in the kitchen. Mel said to her: 'Why don't you sleep?'

Sosi said: 'I just worry too much.'

Mel said: 'How can you make a difference? Can you make any difference?'

Sosi said: 'No, but I can't sleep; I just can't sleep.'

At about 4 o'clock she went to the bedroom and Mel said – and here Sosina raises the pitch of her voice a few notes to indicate that she now knows how he was nuancing the truth – 'Ah, you know, Yonatan rang.'

'What did he say?' she asked.

'Oh,' continued Mel, as if it was nothing very important, 'the doctor wants to talk to us.'

'Maybe it's the drip,' Sosi said. 'I'd better go back to the hospital.'

'No,' said Mel, 'you can go in the morning. I don't think it's anything so serious.'

He sat on the edge of the bed a while. And then, as if he had a thought, he said: 'Maybe I should go. I can go help Yonatan.'

She said, 'Should I come with you?'

'No,' he said, 'You stay here and rest because you've been up all night.'

She sat up on the corner of the bed, unsleeping.

Yonatan had sat up late, watching his father breathing. At one point he dozed off for a few minutes. When he awoke he noticed Tewabé lying very still. A nurse came in to check Tewabé's breathing. She said to Yonatan: 'You see how his eyes are closed? That means he's had a very peaceful death.'

A couple of hours later Sosina heard the car and two sets of footsteps on the front porch. Mel and another person. Yonatan.

'I started crying,' she tells me. 'I knew when I heard both of their footsteps together coming home that he was gone.'

'Mel had already told all of the Ethiopian community,' she says, 'Our friends. So that when he and Yonatan came home at 6 am, all of the other people were waiting outside, too. And they just came in and started to organise the house. They started to organise the kitchen and began to cook. Some people went to the markets and bought meat and vegetables. Some people brought bread, some people drinks. From that point on for the week until we left for Ethiopia the house would be full of people. They did everything for us. And whoever had heard the news would come and put money down in the lounge room, because they know how much it costs to fly his body home.

'Mel and Yonatan knew I didn't want to see him dead. I prefer to remember him alive. That's how it was with Abraham, too. My mum looked at Abraham's dead body and she said, *He looks so thin; he's lost so much weight*. She always has that in her memory. But when I remember Abraham, he is playing football, he is singing, dancing.'

That week Sosina took phone calls from all over the world. 'How's your dad? Can we talk to him?'

'No,' she said, 'You know when he had that operation before and they put him to sleep for a week? They've done that again.'

Even her mum believed her. *What use is the truth,* thought Sosi. *The truth might kill her.*

There is always a right and a wrong time for the truth.
She would hang up the phone and bawl her eyes out.

Sosina texted:
My dad is in heaven…
He passed away 4 am this
morning at western
general hospital,
Melbourne. Pls don't
share this on face book
b/c my mum still doesn't
know :(

14

The arrangements

Four am, local time, an hour south-east of Dubai. Across our four seats on the plane: myself, Sosi, Raeey and Meski, although Raeey wriggles back and forth and swaps places all the time.

I can't quite believe I'm suddenly on a plane to Addis Ababa with Sosina. It is early Friday morning.

On Wednesday evening Linda and I went over to Sosi's house in St Albans to give our condolences for Tewabé's death and make a contribution towards her travel costs, as she and Meski would be accompanying Tewabé's body on the flight to Addis Ababa for his funeral. The house was full of people: friends, acquaintances and others Sosi didn't even know from the local Ethiopian community. Sosi was sitting on the floor in the lounge room with several women friends, a pot of coffee brewing on the burner on the floor.

'Can you come to Addis?' she said to me. 'I think it would be good for you to come. I've talked to Mel; he thinks it's a good idea. It will just be full-on for you. But, if you come,' she continues, 'you should come sooner rather than later so you don't miss anything. We will be arriving on Friday morning and the funeral is on Saturday lunchtime. Really, you should come to the funeral. You would have to leave tomorrow night with us.'

This made absolute sense as soon as she said it, even though I had never before considered it as an option. (I often don't notice things that are staring me in the face.) Less than one day to organise a visa, ticket, insurance, US dollars, and to try to tie up all the loose ends at work, or at least cauterise the gaping wounds. On the way home with Linda, in the car, the two of us made a list. I started calling work colleagues, cancelling meetings. I plotted a path through the next day that began at the Ethiopian consulate in Fitzroy, then involved driving to the university I work at and running to and fro to talk to my boss and to his boss, whose EA had to talk to the EA of her boss's boss and to the EA of her boss's boss's boss (the last boss being the Vice Chancellor and President of the university) all of whom were required to approve my travel, I was told, because Ethiopia is on the Australian Government's list of very scary 'high-risk countries' and since this book was one of my officially sanctioned research activities I needed their approval in order to get travel insurance. Remarkably, thanks to luck and the skills of the various EAs, all the hoops were jumped through in about two hours and I could flee the building in time to arrive at Tewabé's Australian memorial service mid-afternoon.

I scarcely saw Sosina there. She was shrouded in black alongside Meski in the front row of the Ethiopian Orthodox church fashioned from converted schoolrooms on a side street in Melbourne's western suburbs. The women sat on one side of the aisle; the men, the other. The air in the darkened room was thick with incense. Various friends from the circus crowded alongside me in the back row, wearing incongruous suits. The service was conducted

entirely in Amharic. I tried to interpret the various ritual procedures and mentally compared them with those I was familiar with
in Anglo-Australian funerals. There were no eulogies from family
members; the priest ran the whole thing. The sunlight outside
was so bright you could see it forcing its way in around the edges
of the long drapes on the windows. We stood, we sat, we stood,
sat. I tried to be respectful in my ignorance but afterwards bolted
for the door to drive home, pack my bags and hit the freeway for
the airport.

Linda and I arrived on time and waited at the international
departures gate. Sosi and Meski arrived late with an entourage of
farewellers. Mel shook my hand and looked me in the eye: 'It is
going to be hard for you,' he said, somewhat ominously. 'But it
will be a good experience.' He patted me on the arm.

Not for the first time I wondered what exactly I was in for.

Sosi and Meski both look as if they are holding their breath most
of the way across the Indian Ocean.

Sosi has followed a very specific procedure to alert those in
Addis of her father's death. Her mother must not know anything;
this is the first principle. Indeed, Sosi has conspired long-distance
with her mother's doctor to have Ayanalem admitted to hospital
for some tests the day before we are to arrive with Tewabé's body.
Yonatan, who has flown from Melbourne to Addis ahead of us, is
assisting with the general subterfuge. His role has been to prepare
the ground by saying that Tewabé is now gravely ill and has been
given only a fifty-fifty chance of living. Sosi wants to delay the
shock for her mother and have her receive the news in hospital in
case her body takes it badly and she becomes in need of immediate medical attention.

But neither have her sister Israel or her brother Amaha been
told. Instead, as is customary, Sosi has phoned a small number of
elders in her parents' community. One of these is Israel's husband.

He won't tell Israel and Amaha until early in the morning of the Friday we are arriving with the body. In the meantime, he and the other elders will have put in train all the necessary preparations of the *edirr*.

An *edirr* is a traditional form of social insurance, used typically for funerals and weddings. A community of families contribute to its funds, with which essential items such as canvas marquees, seating, trestle tables and durable plastic plates and cups are bought. These items are stored somewhere convenient and brought out as required. When a member of the community dies the elders of the *edirr* mobilise to support the bereaved family: both a financial and a physical contribution is expected.

Before dawn on the day of our arrival with Tewabé's body, the people from the *edirr* will have assembled outside the gates of Ayanalem's house, just as the Ethiopian community did for Sosina back in Melbourne. As soon as the family is informed about the death, the gates will swing open. Work will commence immediately to erect the marquee over the courtyard, line it with benches and prepare food to accommodate and feed the thousands of mourners who will arrive throughout the day as word spreads across the country.

The windows of the bus at Dubai airport, as it wanders across the tarmac along the painted roads to take us from our landed plane to find the terminal, are covered with a kind of variegated screening material that makes the passing airport blurry and indistinct, as if just beyond our jetlagged consciousness. Raeey doesn't mind. She has her wide eyes up against the window, while the rest of us try to find something, anything else, to look at.

In the terminal we go up in one lift, down in another. Up in a third, down in a fourth and a fifth as well. Not because we are lost or have gone the wrong way but because that is the way you get to Gate 118, according to the arrows. In between the various lifts, we walk for half an hour or so, following those arrows. Dubai airport is a chintzy treasure-trove stacked with jewels and sunglasses, Glenfiddich, Pall Mall and Chanel No. 5. Sosi takes the opportunity to buy a portable DVD player for Raeey to watch DVDs on in Addis, since Mel forgot to pick one up at Kmart in Melbourne. The TV won't be switched on at Ayanalem's house for several months, during the grieving times, but she'll be able to sneak the little DVD player on for Raeey.

We go to the café nearest to our gate and order coffee. A friendly German couple who have been on a cruise in the Gulf invite us to share their table. We find out they have a part-time business back home in Bremen based around a portable wine bar they have established in some kind of caravan, which they park alongside Bremen harbour for events and parties. 'We've made a lot of new friends with our caravan,' the husband tells us, 'It's very, how would you say, communitarian?'

'Communal,' I suggest.

Sosi tells them why we are en route to Addis; that we're burying her father. We share our stories, big and small, around this little table, lost in the sumptuous excesses of Dubai International, and make a strangely comforting connection with these people from across the world, whom we will surely never see again. It would be nice to have a gluhwein one day at their Christmas caravan.

I wonder about where I will sleep at Ayanalem's house, and whether I will be so forgotten in the tumult of grief to come that I will have to fend for myself to find food and drink. No doubt these childish anxieties mask a deeper fear of being confronted by the power of grief, and death.

We fly in to Addis across parched fields and hamlets in the lee of rocky bluffs.

Sosi is feeling sick, dreading what's to come, but she does a good job of hiding it from the rest of us.

Everything is sun-bleached. The airport – I realise I have only been here at night before now – looks like it could be built on the edge of the earth. Looking out the windows as we enter the terminal building, only a narrow rim of land can be seen beyond the tarmac, and the modest round hilltops poking up beyond might be islands from a neighbouring world.

As soon as we come down the escalator from the airport gate, before we have reached customs or anything, a tall young woman is there to meet us. She wraps Sosina and Meski in her arms and the three of them are all of a sudden weeping; or, rather, keening in unison, as the escalator chugs its endless curving path behind them. Raeey stands and gazes up at the familiar grown-ups who are breaking into pieces, and I stand, too, as if offstage, helpfully juggling Sosi's extra carry-ons.

After the first wave of mourning has washed through, and their bodies settle into calmness again, the young woman whisks Raeey into her arms and leads us to the customs area, where she is able to take us through without standing in the queues. Sosi and Meski are dressed by this time all in black, with long black headscarves, so I guess it is apparent to the other travellers why we are receiving special treatment.

From customs we go to collect our cases from the carousels and are again whisked to the head of the security screening queue. After Dubai, Addis airport feels small, simple and almost deserted. Ours is the only flight arriving.

Out beyond the barriers, four or five male friends of the family are stationed. As soon as Sosi and Meski see the men they start to cry again, although the word 'cry' hardly hints at what they do. They weep and wail and are wrapped up once more in the embrace of those who have come to take care of them. Every now and then, when Meski's grief is threatening to consume her, the tall woman will speak to her almost sharply: 'Meski! Meski!' As if to pull her back from the precipice.

In the glaring sun of the carpark we wait by one of the cars. Sosina packs all of Raeey's many belongings onto one airport trolley. Sosi's best friend from childhood, Ferahiwot (Feray for short) is here to take Raeey away to her place for a few days. Feray has two children of her own. Raeey can be distracted and happy there, and Sosi won't have to worry about her while she needs to concentrate her energies on the funeral and her mother.

After some debate in the carpark it is agreed that Sosi, Meski and I will all be driven in one car to Ayanalem's house. Addis this time feels familiar, although I still can't take my bearings on any landmarks, and in fact the airport seems to have been moved closer to the town (this can't be true). The streets are full of activity: people strolling and bustling. A woman and her friend kiss goodbye on a street corner as if they won't be seeing each other again for ages or as if they are acting in a movie. We pass modest shopfronts painted in faded pastel colours perhaps inspired by the Italians: pinks, lime greens and powder blues. Sosi and Meski, sitting in the back seat, are quiet and calm, building up their strength again for mourning. A gold-statued figure in a roadside park holds up a cross; he might be Jesus, or St George. He's pointing in the direction we are heading.

The tall building on the corner, which was under construction last time (the ship of flapping blue plastic), has been completed. Its gleaming newness is already becoming dusty. Ayanalem and Tewabé's street is now paved, miraculously, allowing us to travel along it approximately ten times faster than before, too quickly to notice if everything's still there: the tiny bar where Sosi's alcoholic friend hung out, the even tinier shanty shack by the roadside near the culvert, or the woodyard selling slender eucalypt logs.

Here we are already outside the compound. I see the familiar Pepsi signs handpainted on the café verandah walls. The café is closed. The car pulls up to a halt on the opposite side of the road. The courtyard has been covered over with canvas, forming a dark tunnel the mouth of which is choked with people wrapped in white blankets. They all look over in our direction. They have been waiting for us. A man among them steps out and begins to hop around as if the tarmac beneath him is suddenly too hot to rest his feet upon. He's dancing and singing an impromptu song and dance of grief. The crowd around him hums and lists with its own modulations of despair. Sosi leans over and murmurs to me, 'You wait here, Dave.' She hands me an envelope full of American dollars: 'You look after our money, keep it safe.'

The driver repeats: 'Wait here. When it is a good time, I will come back and get you.'

Sosi and Meski get out of the car, and in that moment as they cross the street I watch their bodies scissor inwards. They bow and bend and empty out their lungs, are sucked into the navel of the crowd and gone, the crowd closing over and swirling in behind them. All around, on the street, passers-by and neighbours have stopped to stare or pay their respects, or both. I am alone in the front seat of the old Toyota but nobody stares at me today, despite my lathered-on whiteness. It is peaceful there, comforting to be absolutely useless. After what seems to be a long time (perhaps ten minutes), the driver reappears. He strides purposefully across the road, as if a plainclothes cop in some Friday-night drama, and opens my door. 'You can go in now.' Together we wrestle my suitcase from the boot. I take one of Sosi's cases, too. Now I feel I'm doing something useful. I have been elevated to the status of a featured cameo, as we push our way through the crowd, and I'm careful not to stare back at all those looking at me. I must be some friend of Sosina's from Australia. I suppose that's who I am.

Who knows what happens next. I think I'm taken directly to my room – the hotel room I will sleep in. It is quite bare, almost like a prison cell to look at, but with cartoon condoms on the windows, and to me it is the most beautiful room I've ever seen because it's mine, every inch of it, in this place where I don't know the first thing about anything at all. Soon, someone knocks, and I'm taken through the crowds in the bigger courtyard into the small courtyard and up the few stairs into Ayanalem's room, where Sosi and Meski have joined their family (except Ayanalem herself, who's still in hospital). I sit on a chair. Even now, as always, I am a favoured guest in this house of politeness that has become a house of ordered wailing, the grievers and the comforters taking turns to swap their roles.

Sosina recounts story after story of the last six months.

Some time later, Tewabé's coffin arrives and is laid to rest on the table in the lounge room, covered with a cloth and a wreath of flowers. In the corner above the couch, where the TV would normally be, two framed photographs of handsome young men are propped up side by side behind a lighted candle. One of them is Tewabé. 'Who's the other one?' I ask Sosina.

'That's my brother who died. Abraham.'

The last time they had a funeral.

'As a child and a young man,' Sosi says, 'Abraham was the comedian in the family.' Of all the family, she and he were closest, she tells me. His is the story always waiting first and last.

Abraham lived six years in Cairo among the Ethiopian refugee community. Waiting in the 'queue' – as if there is a queue. He helped a lot of other Ethiopian refugees while he was there, Sosi tells me. He used to take them to the Ethiopian Orthodox Church for solace, and he'd help them with their refugee claims and immigration cases.

The United Nations granted him his refugee status early on, but Australia wouldn't take him. The humanitarian intake favoured women and children, not single young men. Three times Sosina went through all the rigmarole of applying to the Australian

Government for permission to bring Abraham to Australia as a refugee. Each time it cost her $2000 for the lawyers. Each time she waited for eighteen months before receiving a form letter of rejection. *Your application is not successful.* (No reasons given.) For six years she worked on Abraham's case. After the third rejection she found a social worker called Ron in Melbourne who began to help her. Ron knew how to approach the Immigration Department; how to make them listen. They arranged a date for a new interview for Abraham with the Australian authorities in Cairo.

But in the meantime Abraham ran out of hope.

'The Australian interview is coming up,' said Sosi. 'They will say yes this time; we have Ron's help. I know it will work this time, Abraham.'

'I can't wait another two months,' he told her. 'I am dying here.'

She hung there on the line. What could she promise, really?

Six weeks later he was dead.

There are things about this story too difficult to tell. What I can say is that Abraham picked up a gun and shot himself in front of his girlfriend. She was about to go out, even though it was late at night, because she worked night shifts.

He had changed into his pyjamas.

'Don't go, please,' he said. 'I don't want you to go tonight.'

And she said: 'No, no, I have to go.'

And he said: 'Please don't go.'

But she said: 'No, no, I have to go.'

(In Sosi's version of the story there is this repetition in their dialogue, which might reflect the way she heard the story or might be a little loop she puts in herself to try to hold onto that moment of before it was too late, to try to see inside those simple words, the type of everyday words that gather around a crisis. *Please don't go. No, no, I have to go.*)

He took out the gun. His girlfriend thought it was a toy.

He pointed the gun at his head and said: 'Don't scream. Look after my mother.'

...and she was like: Oh, my God, please don't...

...but he was already gone.

None of which would ever make any sense. Not to Sosina. Not to anyone. At some point, things no longer do make sense. I know this because of my father.

Abraham's death happened only two weeks after Sosi and Mel's wedding celebrations in September 2005. They had gone back to Addis Ababa for ceremonies and parties and it was there that they heard the news.

'When my brother Abraham died,' she says, 'I hardly slept any night; I felt like I was running while I was sleeping, but I would wake up full of energy. Still running. I lost a lot of weight. Too much energy, everything going very fast. My hair growing very quickly, my nails growing very quickly, but brittle, hollow, breaking. Too fast. I went to the doctor; he gave me a blood test. What should have been twenty-seven on the scale was fifty-six. My thyroid was producing too much – too much hormone, maybe, too much something. The doctor said they could take the thyroid out but then I would have to take medicine all my life. Or I could take this other medicine; hope that it got better. I had three pills a day to start with. It helped. I slowed down. I was lucky: my thyroid stabilised when I became pregnant with Raeey.

'If it ever comes back I'll take the pills again. If I feel I'm speeding up too much.'

She says: 'I googled *hyperthyroid*: it happens when you're devastated. When you lose a family member. I was sick for a long time but Circus Oz said: *We will keep your job. Don't worry: you can come back when you want.* At least that was one thing I didn't have to worry about. I was away from work for seven, eight months. Three months in Addis and then back home in Melbourne.'

Then as now, Sosina and Mel borrowed thousands of dollars to fly their loved one's body home to Ethiopia to be buried.

Then as now, the *edirr* was notified and it assembled outside the gates of Ayanalem and Tewabé's house before dawn, bringing breakfast and everything else required along with the bad news.

'Who killed him?' said Tewabé, anguished, sitting in the lounge room. His best friend went close to him and murmured: 'No, I heard he killed himself.'

On Saturday, the day of Tewabé's funeral, I wake at 3 am to the sound of chanting. These are the priests assembled around Tewabé's coffin in the lounge room. Their chanting, deep and mellifluous, continues for another hour then ebbs away. The cat stops wailing. The roosters stop crowing. Only distant dogs bark and howl. The house breathes.

In the morning I get up and sit for a while in the courtyard, watching the water being lugged in from an old Land Rover in a range of plastic containers. The mains water is not running. Nobody knows why.

I am invited into Ayanalem's room, where the five siblings, Sosina, Amaha, Yonatan, Meski and Israel, joined by various cousins, aunts and uncles, are discussing how best to break the news to Ayanalem at the hospital. Before long, charged with this responsibility, Sosi and Yonatan set off with Amaha in his car.

I sit on the bar terrace drinking coffee, staying out of the way.

Later I am invited to join the crowd assembling in the courtyard, who sit along the benches packed in under the canvas, wrapped in shawls and blankets. Their hum of mourning is very gradually rising in intensity. Emuye, the woman Sosi calls the chef, appears in our midst – Emuye of the skinny frame and jumbled teeth who more than anyone apart from Ayanalem keeps the entire household running. Uncharacteristically, she takes centre stage here to express a grief so profound that it propels her into hopping and whirling,

doubling over repeatedly, directing a circle of unanswerable questions to individuals seated along the rows. She is followed shortly
afterwards by Sosina's sister, Israel, and several of the cousins who
had been in Ayanalem's room, each of them taking their turn as
impromptu soloists within this finely tuned orchestra of loss. I
am like a piece of driftwood washed up here. I can only absorb
so much, although I try. Their expression of grief, volcanic as it
is, is no more or less culturally ritualised than the stiff-shouldered
shuffling, neatly bowed heads and discreet tears of a funeral in
my Anglo-Saxon culture. But is this healthier? To expunge, expel,
release, disgorge, let all the demons and the sorrows fly. Rather
than to flatline and to swallow, to grind up half-formed cries...
to keep a lid on it...I would like to learn this way of mourning;
I would like to be able to do it. To be able, as the chef has done
just now, to dance around like a pork chop, emitting any and all of
my uncensored feelings (at least it looks convincingly uncensored)
in front of anyone and everyone, and then to sit down on a chair,
catch my breath, collect myself and have a quiet chat to the person
sitting next to me. It seems quite healthy.

As for Sosi, she's a proud woman of her culture and not
backward with her mourning but she does say, 'They go on a
bit sometimes.'

Given the wild grieving, one after another, of the chef, Israel
and the cousins, I begin to wonder if there has been some terrible
news from hospital; if Ayanalem herself, upon hearing the news
of Tewabé's passing, has succumbed to the weakness in her heart,
as each of her children fears she will. But after a while, as the
intensity of this latest, most terrible episode fades, I come to think
that, on the contrary, they were all taking the opportunity to
scream and shout and flail about *before* Ayanalem arrived home,
because they would need to hold themselves strong in front of her.

All morning the tension in the compound grows as we wait for
the family to return. The crowd, which by now numbers several

hundred, has stilled. Everyone has taken to their own concave thoughts. I find a spot to perch on the low wall between the courtyard and the restaurant, by the sidewall of the marquee and a portrait of Tewabé as a young man. From here I can see across the crowded courtyard to the front gate and the street beyond, now thick with people. In the middle of the road the *edirr* has erected a second, freestanding marquee, from where they will serve lunch after the funeral. Tewabé's best friend, Gazahin, wearing a baseball cap, is quietly stage-managing things (just as Tewabé would have done for him), directing the arrival of guests, vehicles and deliveries.

Finally a ripple of commotion sweeping in from the road heralds the arrival of Amaha's car. It turns in through the gate. A hand waves out the passenger front window, not to any of us but outstretched to the sky above, as if to clutch at the hand of the husband floating away from her towards God. Everyone stands up as the car edges its way forward. Benches are picked up and swept to the side and the crowd parts to give the car a path through, as far as it can come towards the house. I can now see Ayanalem spread across the front seat, wailing. Sosina, Yonatan and Meski emerge from the rear. They have to get oxygen to their mother from a small tank, so that her breathing can be strong enough for her to stand up out of the car and take the few steps through the inner courtyard to her bedroom. The pressing crowd is broken and agitated. It looks for a moment as if it is going to flood in after her and drown her with its grief. But like a miracle a grey-bearded holy man appears, holding up a small Ethiopian cross and wearing the round cap and fine robes of the church. The family's local priest.

He speaks briefly to the crowd by the Corolla, striking, with his firm, even tone, a note of authority that seems to come not from his office alone but from some great strength of character that is either a natural talent or a well-honed skill. He says to the crowd: 'Stop! You must stop now! Get a grip! You must be strong now; can't you see that this woman, this family need you to be strong!' Or something to that effect — I scarcely need a translator.

As if they've been collectively slapped, the crowd comes to its senses.

I am thinking (and I bet Sosi is thinking): *At least Ayanalem was able to stand and cry out. She has made it this far.*

Amaha reappears to unpack the rest of the luggage from the hospital, and to back the car the short distance out across the loose volcanic rock of the courtyard to park it in the street. The benches and mourners flow back into the space the car had occupied so that within moments the courtyard has returned to its original formation: blanketed and shrouded, brooding. Latecomers are directed to the tables of the closed restaurant at the rear.

Since a number of people close to the family are now flowing into the inner courtyard, I take the opportunity to follow them, thinking I might have a chance to pay my own last respects to Tewabé, lying in the coffin with a single candle burning at its head. The unadorned inner courtyard — where they wash the dishes in plastic containers on the ground, where they killed a sheep last time I was here — is crowded with people standing, watching. I don't follow those entering the lounge room; it is as if to go in there requires a pitch of emotional intensity I can't rise to.

All of a sudden six pallbearers from the funeral service march in, their skinny young bodies lost in splendidly bright and vastly oversized blue uniforms, their matching shiny oversized peaked caps reminiscent of those worn by pantomime policemen. With a minimum of fuss and no ceremony at all they lift the red cloth–wrapped coffin from its resting place and manoeuvre it backwards into the internal courtyard, squeezing the crowd aside to make room, reversing as they clear the doorway and scrambling to get a better grip while keeping at bay a frenzied young man who seems to want to fling himself on top. Picking up speed, the pallbearers disappear around the corner with their cargo. The rest of us stream behind. Evidently the funeral procession is underway. I see Yonatan ahead of me so, having no idea where we are going, I decide to follow him, guessing, correctly as it turns out, that Sosina will not be walking with the funeral procession but staying behind to look after her mother.

We flow out toward the street, where the pallbearers can be seen depositing the coffin carefully in the back of a black hearse bedecked on either side with bright orange reefs of flowers woven onto bamboo frames. The pallbearers arrange themselves in irregular marching positions in front of the hearse as it takes off. One carries a framed portrait of Tewabé in front of his chest so that anyone we pass along the way can see whose death is being mourned today by this long procession of several thousand friends, neighbours, relatives, colleagues and acquaintances, walking on the newly sealed road up the hill towards the distant church.

I soon lose Yonatan in the crowd and settle into walking by myself. It feels as if most people are glad to be strolling in the sunshine, after the closeness and tension of the long wait in the courtyard. People chat in twos and threes as they walk, the women raising parasols. I am glad of my hat under the high-altitude sun of Addis. An orange-shirted team of teenage boys are playing a yellow-shirted team on the dirt soccer field as we pass by. The people of the neighbourhood stand outside their tiny shops, under trees or against the fences of house compounds to watch us. As if in a dream or a South American novel, we follow the hearse around one corner and the next, our procession extending and diluting itself in the busy streets so that I have to take care to follow the mourners ahead of me, dressed up in their best shawls and dresses and carrying their parasols, since I have no idea where we are going and could easily drift off into the dusty streets of Addis carrying no address or phone number, no way at all of finding my way home.

After an eternity, the hearse turns off the bitumen roads and heads up a steep lane, at the top of which an arched entrance presages the church complex. The basic tin houses of slums line the lane. Rocky paths disappear between them. From a doorway, three ragged kids check us out.

The hearse drives around to the rear of the large central church and we all follow, but no sooner have they started to unload the coffin and carry it up the church steps than they are stopped. It becomes apparent that there has been a misunderstanding by the funeral service and we are supposed to be at a different church further up the hill and on the other side of the graveyard. Everyone takes this in good spirits. The team reverses the coffin into the hearse and points the crowd of mourners along an old narrow path that leads through the graveyard.

Along the path we file past a group of people described in my notes afterwards as 'several poor souls, sitting in the shade'. I'm not sure why it is here in particular that language failed and fails me – I'm tempted simply to erase these people because I can't find the right tone or tenor to speak about them. It shouldn't be that hard. They're not begging but they're surely desperate and homeless and here for the sanctuary of the church. Who knows what their story is? In writing they stop me in my tracks, because in reality I step right by them, I suppose.

The stone path dips away down a slope. On either side graves appear to have been dug up or at least disturbed. The graveyard is shaded with tall old trees, unusual for Addis Ababa: cedars and an orange flowering tree I have never seen before. A tightly woven bird's nest hangs from a branch like an earring. We pick our way down the rough path and across a dry creek to a wider track, which leads up to another arched entranceway heralding a church. The courtyard inside is already packed with mourners. To enter the church itself we have to climb two flights of concrete steps as if entering an old school building or a block of flats.

Inside the church the coffin has been laid to rest to one side. A frenzied knot of mourners jumps up and down and caterwauls in front of it until a guy with a microphone insists they calm down. Attendants distribute and light long orange beeswax candles that burn hungrily in our hands. A circle of brightly coloured priests chant in a swirl around the coffin.

Before long the coffin is picked up again and carried out and down the same steps we came up. We all stream out behind in something of a crush, and watch as the coffin is deposited inside a large undercroft. I can't see inside past the throng of people but it becomes clear that this is the end of today's ceremonies pertaining to the coffin. Now everyone watches a group of scrappily dressed men dancing, jumping and crying in a circle in the courtyard, slapping their bodies with their hands in sorrowful ecstasy. I wonder who these people are, barefoot and ragged, that look so different from the mourners at large. Local people who join in on passing funerals for some reason of their own? Later I learn that they are relatives of Tewabé who have travelled into the city from the countryside, arriving on a bus early this morning, and that this is their traditional form of grieving.

On the way back from the church, some of the mourners depart from the main track, taking a shortcut through the grave-yard. I follow them and find myself stepping through a shady grove of graves along a ridge. Each grave features a headstone with hand-painted writing in Amharic and, above this writing, a small photograph of the face of the deceased set into an oval glass frame. The faces look out into the graveyard blindly, some young, some old, all looking healthy and surely never thinking at the moment they were photographed that one day this particular image of them would be set in stone to face the weather of the passing seasons, sentinel to their own mortal remains, consigned on this hillside here to watch and wait for old friends and relations to come by and talk to them and cry over their memory.

The crowds of mourners return to Ayanalem's house, forming a long orderly queue down the middle of the road, to be served lunch by the men and women of the *edirr*. They have set up the trestle tables in a marquee outside.

Injera, *wat* and orange cordial for all.

Throughout the funeral, Sosina stays inside, watching over her mother's grief. She doesn't need to be there for the funeral. She knows it will go smoothly; finally, she's not required. Others can run the show. She doesn't need to see him buried. She needs to see her mother living.

15

On the terrace

The following morning I think I can hear the priests chanting together in the lounge room again, where the casket had lain. But when I go outside the house is dark, the courtyard empty, the front gate locked, even the little gate to the inner courtyard swung shut in a gesture I take to mean 'Do not disturb'. Perhaps I had been dreaming? I return to my bedroom, lie down on the single bed and listen. The sound of the Muslim call to prayer from a nearby mosque begins to fill the silence. A chorus of howling is set off from dog to dog to dog across the neighbourhood. I close my eyes again.

Sometime after 6 am the front gates to the streets must be opened because the sounds of distressed mourners are once again resonating against the steel of my bedroom door, and the corridor is bustling with keys and footsteps as preparations for the new day of grieving gets into full swing.

Breakfast is a plate of scrambled eggs and fresh bread shared with Sosina. The chef, Emuye, now has a younger sister who helps out, in place of the assistant who was here last time I visited. The younger sister brings the water jug and soap for us to wash our hands. She had been living with another family previously, Sosi tells me, but they never educated her. When she turned 13 or 14 she would most likely have been raped, so Tewabé invited her to shelter with his family and help out while she went to school.

Many of the mourners remain at Ayanalem's place for days after the funeral. After the first three days, the *edirr* packs up the marquee in the courtyard and things start to look more normal, although the café and restaurant remain closed. But for weeks and months, Sosi says, people will keep arriving, as those in remote towns or just returned from overseas hear about Tewabé's death. At any time, a person might walk in the front gate and start to wail and cry. He will be ushered through the courtyards to pay his respects to Ayanalem and her family, and afterwards invited to sit down in the lounge room to collect himself, reminisce and share some food.

Sosi is often busy greeting guests or looking after her mum, who lies grieving and bereft in her bed. Ayanalem breaks periodically into disconsolate keening, calling out to Tewabé and to God. Sosi is always at pains to try to keep her as calm as possible, to protect her fragile lungs and heart. I spend a lot of time on the terrace of the restaurant learning card games, listening to Yonatan and his male cousins talk politics and philosophy.

There are more than sixty political parties in Ethiopia and the government is doing a good job building a multi-party system, declares one cousin. Yonatan translates for me.

Another rolls his eyes and comments: 'He's only saying that because he *works* for the government!'

A cousin who has just finished a degree in economics launches into a dissertation on the effects of the devaluation of the Ethiopian birr, which I find impossible to follow.

Yonatan, the expat, is a critic.

'When I left Ethiopia in 2006 it was the fourth poorest country in the world; now it is the second poorest,' he tells them.

They all find this hard to believe.

'I don't see how it can be the fourth poorest country—'

'—Second poorest,' he corrects.

'—Because there is a lot of growth now, a lot of development.'

'Yes, the government builds infrastructure, I agree, you can see it everywhere. Roads and buildings.'

'And bridges.'

'Yes, of course, and bridges,' agrees Yonatan. 'But you can't eat a building. You can't eat a road. Seventy per cent of the people are poor; they don't have enough to eat.'

'What about Somalia?' asks another cousin, 'That must be poorer!'

Yonatan scoffs. 'Somalia is not even a country. It's chaos.'

'The government here is better than the previous governments, I agree,' concedes Yonatan, 'The president is a smart man, he is trying...'

In the morning, on the terrace, Sosina's cousin Gaito asks me, out of the blue: 'Why is it so much harder to go to Australia than to America or Canada or Britain or other countries?'

I'm surprised at this. 'Is that what people find in Ethiopia?' I ask.

'Yes,' he says. 'If someone says to you he is immigrating to Australia you will go, *Wow!*'— He makes an expression of great surprise —'Whereas if someone says he is immigrating to America you will be like this,' He makes an expression that means: *Well, not bad.*

'Why is it so hard to go to Australia?' he repeats, not accusatory, simply curious.

I had no idea that was the case. I had thought they would be all equally hard to get to. *What could be a good answer to that question?* I ask myself. I feel like I should have one.

He has a thought: 'Is it because there is not very much land in Australia?'

'No,' I say, 'there is a lot of land...'

Another time I am sitting having lunch with Yonatan and a group of eight or so young men, Yonatan's friends and relations, in a restaurant. Lunch that day is *injera*, as usual, but with a creamy vegetarian *wat* and a cabbage dish instead of the usual meaty fare.

'Why are we fasting today?' I ask. Every Wednesday and Friday, I have learned, are days designated for *fasting*, which, according to the prescription of the Coptic Orthodox Church, means eating only vegan food. But today is not a Wednesday or a Friday.

One of the men, Andnet, embarks upon an explanation, which Yonatan translates. It begins like this: *The sky and earth were fighting. God created Adam and Hewon*...and proceeds from there on a long and winding path through the Old Testament towards Jesus. (People still have time to talk over lunch in Ethiopia.) The details of the account are often challenged and debated by the other guys, one of whom periodically calls up expert advice from his girlfriend or his sister on his mobile phone, so as to bolster his position vis-a-vis the precise chain of events.

It strikes me as I listen to them and feverishly scribble down notes that the long answer to my question is not to them metaphorical but literal: an explanation of the facts behind the nature of today's lunch. I am an atheist; to me the Christian God is a convenient and comforting (for some) mythological construct, rather than the founder and ruler of the universe. But they aren't trying to persuade me of their faith, or sharing their beliefs: they are simply relating a true story.

Anthropologists might, in earlier times at least, have considered this type of discourse a *mythology*. For hundreds of years white people have been studying black people and the funny things they say. But my hosts turn the questioning back on me. When they find out I have no religion and don't believe in any god, they look at me with, variously, curiosity, surprise or amusement (and a fair smattering of pity all round). They pose a number of simple questions designed to reveal the flaws in my thinking.

'Who created the world?'

'Nobody.'

'Well, then, how did the world begin?'

I shuffle my brain to that particular folder and find it rather thin. Well…the Big Bang. That explains it. That is clearly, unequivocally the answer. Lock it in. I am confident the scientists know what they're talking about. I take them on faith, actually, in this instance, but I do have confidence in the logic of the scientific method and peer review and, well, generally, the march of knowledge.

But how to explain this to a bunch of doubters?

I lift my hands in front of me to shape something like an imaginary bowling ball. 'Well,' I say, 'in the beginning the entire universe was very small…'

'Like a ball?' Yonatan tries to help.

'Yes, kind of like a ball,' I say, realising I have no idea what is supposed to be between my hands. 'And then it…kind of…all started expanding…really quickly…there was a huge explosion… They call it the Big Bang…'

They all just look at me.

Whose idea was it to give such a childish kind of name to the inaugurating event of the universe? I'm now thinking. God wouldn't be so stupid.

I move my hands away from each other as if the imaginary bowling ball is being inflated like a balloon, to demonstrate the action of the Big Bang. I think to myself: *I believe I know this to be true, and usually I live in a particular slice of the Western world where, by and large, this is taken for granted.* But at the same time I think to myself: *If I was hearing this, and I was one of my Ethiopian hosts, I can see why I might find it difficult to swallow the idea that the universe began as a bowling ball that one day exploded.* Much more difficult than to believe that Haile Selasse was a direct descendant of the Queen of Sheba. Just for instance.

Shortly after we arrive back at Ayanalem's house, three old women come in, wailing loudly. After their tears have subsided they sit and talk intently with Sosina, so intently that I'm dying to know what they're talking about. Finally Sosina pauses to fill me in.

'They told me the most amazing story,' she says. 'Of what happened yesterday in the countryside where my dad grew up. All the people from the district gathered together. They sent the young boys out with bells to spread the word. They came together in a huge field, much more people than were here in Addis. They made a coffin and covered it in cloth and they hung up some of Tewabé's clothes to represent him, and they made the mourning ceremony around it.'

The women told Sosina that the people chanted: 'You were so strong, Tewabé. I can't believe that you would ever go,' and they clapped hands and danced from foot to foot in the traditional way, all day long.

'You should've seen it, Sosina,' said one of the old women. 'You should have filmed it. You will never see anything like that again.'

Later, Sosina and I are eating ravioli and lasagna at the Zola Italian restaurant in Addis. Sosi is telling me about her dream to return to Addis and set up a circus and dance school and an agency for Ethiopian artists and performers seeking international gigs. We are ruing the fact that the restaurant has closed down its espresso machine before lunch.

Sosi misses Ethiopian culture so much, she says, how strongly families are connected here...She would like to be here to take care of her mother, and most of all for Raeey to be able to grow up with a 'free' life surrounded by family and cousins, as Sosina did herself. She feels so much part of this place and of its culture.

'If I had grown up in Australia,' she says, 'I'm sure I wouldn't feel how I do; I wouldn't care so strongly for looking after my parents.'

Obviously she's thinking about how Raeey will grow up and what is best for her.

'What do you think is good about Australian culture?' I ask her. This stops her. She has to think.

'*Give it a go*,' she offers. '*Take it easy*—?'

She values these quintessentially Australian attitudes. But at first, this seems to be about all that comes to mind.

'The thing is,' she ponders, 'when I think of Australian culture, there is nothing there.'

By which she means, I suppose, that Australian culture is a shallow mélange, or to put it more kindly – how exactly to put it more kindly? A lively mongrel brew of many different cultures, floating like oil atop the deep waters of the indigenous?

I think afterwards that Sosi's offhand comment is not likely to go down well with Australian readers, no matter how worldly and open-minded or self-critical they are. The ingrate! We give her asylum, make her a citizen! We make her Young Victorian of the Year! Nominate her for Young Australian of the Year!

But sitting there in Addis, I find myself hard-pressed to leap to the defence of Australian culture (even though my Ethiopian lasagna's not really up to scratch). All the arguments I can muster as to why living in Australia might be better for her and her family than living in Ethiopia are based on the benefits of comparative wealth: the better health and education systems, the freedom and opportunities to travel.

But then her eyes light up.

'I—love—Melbourne culture!' she says. 'I *love* Melbourne!'

'What? What do you mean Melbourne culture?'

'The coffee shops, the shopping – all the little boutiques! The horseracing! The Grand Prix! I love the way people dress up especially for all of these events. I love all the different cultures. I miss the Asian food of Melbourne so much; the Footscray markets, the fresh vegetables!'

And this makes me think that, when I get home, if the weather is nice one Sunday, we should cycle, Linda, the kids and I, along the Merri Creek and the Yarra River to Richmond to eat pho.

Culture's in the small things. Somewhere in the in-between of deep connections and the mongrel brew. Sosi and I: stepping towards each other.

The third or fourth day after we arrive in Addis, there is still no running water at Ayanalem's house. Sosi and I, spoiled Westerners, are not exactly loving splashing ourselves with cold water and flushing the loo with a bucket, so Sosi offers to take me back to the Sheraton for a shower. The most expensive shower in the country – perhaps in all of Africa.

Sosi loves to avail herself of the Sheraton's plump white towels and manicured attendants every once in awhile. Once again, she puts on her best diamante sunnies and her fake designer handbag and strolls in with me in tow. Today, as she disappears into a shower complex I'm sure is impossibly vast and steamy, I elect once more for the outdoor pool experience. The pool is not so much kidney-shaped as homage to an entire digestive system. It is perfectly the same as when we left it two years ago, replete with extras – white guys slowly chewing on pizzas on banana loungers, bikinied girls prone behind sunglasses, little black kids splashing happily beside their potbellied fathers, waiters glid-ing like dragonflies – just like a scene from *The Truman Show*. I realise that, having forked out the equivalent of one of the waiter's monthly pay cheques for the privilege of swimming, I've forgotten my bathers. Pretending to be undeterred, I wrap myself in a towel and slip into the pool in a quiet corner wearing Ray-Bans and black underpants, and projecting an aura both quietly chic and international. Afterwards I order a pile of berries and whipped cream from a banana lounge and fatten myself up until Sosi arrives.

Later I slip upstairs to visit the travel agent, to enquire about flights to Lalibela. Like everything else at the Sheraton, doing this is a much calmer and easier experience than it would be in real-world Addis.

Ever since Sosi told me about Tewabé's deathbed hallucinations, in which he imagined himself returning to this holy site of pilgrimage and chatting with the priests, I had hoped that we could go there. It is written up in the travel guides as one of the greatest historical sites on Earth. *Come and see twelve stone churches cut intricately and precisely into the bedrock 900 years ago.*

I find out that Lalibela is only a relatively cheap two-hour flight north of Addis. Sosi's never been before; she's never had much chance to be a tourist in Ethiopia. We could go up on a Saturday morning and stay two nights, leaving Raeey with Sosi's friend Feray, removing ourselves for a couple of days from the stresses (for Sosi) and the claustrophobia (for me) of Ayanalem's house in mourning. It would be an adventure and a pilgrimage, a journey together just for the two of us.

In the taxi I pitch the idea to Sosi. She will talk to her mum, and to her brothers and sister, who will have to look after her mum, and to her friend Feray, who will look after Raeey, and if everyone is happy she will say yes. Finally, after this long year of fighting to care for her father and her mother, she can have a weekend off. And she would love to see this famous place, one of the wonders of the world; this place that drew her thoroughly modern father to travel again and again for days on rough roads in order to reach it.

We are all set: we are going to Lalibela.

First stop is Feray's house. Feray lives on the other side of Addis, with her American husband Eric, in a rich area popular

with expats. We will sleep there overnight before our early morning flight, and leave Raeey with her. Amaha drives us there in
the ever-dependable Corolla, past the enormous new buildings
funded by the Chinese for the headquarters of the African Union,
which, along with its predecessor, the Organisation of African
Unity (OAU), Ethiopia has proudly hosted in Addis Ababa for
50 years, down the smooth new bitumen roads sticky-taped across
the city. Amaha laughs, as he ducks down another shortcut, 'There
is a saying: I know Addis so well that I can disappear inside its
mouth and emerge out of its asshole.'

We come to an area of compounds with high walls topped
with barbed wire and fronted by guards. Not prisons – houses.
Upper middle-class normality. Feray's house is at the end of a
laneway, looking out above a beautiful valley that, according to
Eric, is, despite appearances, roamed by gangs of criminals.

We sit out on the terrace of Feray and Eric's charming 1960s-
era home, sipping beer Eric has infused with lemon. The sun is
setting behind the eucalyptus trees on the ridge across the valley.
A group of teenage boys are playing soccer on the dusty ledge of
land directly beyond the high brick wall that protects the property.

It's all quite strange. It's almost as if I am back in a rich country.
The house is like something from the suburbs of my childhood
in Perth, like something from an old American sitcom. Sitting up
here with Eric, suddenly we are two white guys having a beer
together, and Eric is saying how you have to have the barbed
wire and the guard dogs because thieves will come in, given half
a chance, and steal stupid things like the washing off the line or a
hubcap off the car or anything left lying around in the garden. 'A
plastic bucket, for God's sake, as if it's a diamond heist.'

He's saying how there are people called Kuralio who come
by every few months to buy up all of the used whiskey bottles,
jars and cans so that they can resell them at Mercato, the biggest
market in all of Africa, where no household item is too humble to

be resold. Then there are the mop men, who you see wandering the streets selling mops and brooms. They'll knock from time to time and call out through the wall. Everyone knows that back in the Mengistu days many of the mop men were recruited as spies for the government.

He's saying how there was a story all over the papers recently about some guys who stole a large quantity of waste cooking oil from a factory. They took it to a house they rented, got young kids to stomp on it (I'm not sure why), bottled it up and sold it as brand-new cheap cooking oil. Three or four hundred poor people died of poisoning.

Ethiopians, he goes on, are their own worst enemy. They can never be bothered to do things properly. A guy sitting on a huge pile of shit will be proud as anything! Eric married an Ethiopian, he loves the culture, all of that, and he'll criticise his own country just as hard, no problem, but he's still solidly American. 'Here,' he says, 'if a wolf jumps out in front of their car they think it's bad luck. So they won't support the fight to save the critically endangered Ethiopian wolf!' On the other hand, he must admit he kind of admires their pride. One of the few African countries never seriously colonised, all of that. Ethiopians, he has noticed, don't think of themselves as Africans. They call other Africans Africans.

Eric works as a biology teacher at the most exclusive international school in town. He's affable and full of stories, keen to have someone to talk to outside the restricted circles of his life here: the clammy expat community radiating from the school on the one side; Feray's extended family on the other.

Down below in the extensive gardens, Eric has laid out a large series of vegetable beds and is tutoring the family's gardeners in what to grow and when. Right now every bed is full of spring onions, which, Eric insists, is not quite what he had in mind.

It's all so neocolonial and of course I get to both soak up the tranquillity and highlight the ironies afterwards. Raeey and

Feray's kids are running around in the lounge room, using the couch as a trampoline and ignoring the afternoon British children's show subtitled in Arabic because it's beamed in from Dubai. Sosi and Feray are catching up about all the ins and outs of their lives. If you're upper middle class in Addis, as Feray and Eric are because of Eric's well-paid job, you can afford to have domestic staff – cooks, gardeners, guards – and pay them well above the norm. Sosi looks at Feray's life and thinks of the advantages there could be to living here if she and Mel between them had a good job: to be wrapped again in her huge extended family, but also to be able to afford to have help at home so that she could work on all of her plans. The circus school, the agency for performers; a way to build upon all of the opportunities she had at Circus Ethiopia – but this time with police checks.

I was growing comfortable with Eric and the beers, sitting on the patio. But it was impossible for me to imagine the reality of life below the surface here.

At night, Eric says, you often hear hyenas prowling through the valley. They set the dogs off, barking one after the other along their path. This is how you can follow their movements. In the long dry months, says Eric, the hyenas take to the city's drains, criss-crossing its gizzards, open-mouthed and never fussy. They slip along the veins and cracks beneath the city even as it tips further into modernity.

At a summer party on a terrace overlooking a glistening ocean outside Melbourne, in the weeks before Tewabé died, a new friend said to me: 'I know this is very un-PC of me to say but I can't help thinking about your friend: you know, sometimes these people get an idea that Western medicine will be the saviour, but perhaps she would have been better to leave him in his own country with his own traditions and practices?'

She had been quick to draw a moral from the story.

It is easy to read the story of Tewabé's death in Australia as a tragedy, or as a precautionary tale to argue that Sosi somehow overreached in devoting all these resources and energies to an ultimately doomed effort to save him; that in retrospect it would have been better for him to stay in Addis and die at home. Sosi has spent a year of her life, and racked up debts so high she doesn't even want to think about them. As an Australian friend of hers asked her: 'Do you think it's worth it?'

Sosi has no doubts at all. She'll pay off the debts somehow, sooner or later. At least she knows she did everything she could. It's not as if Tewabé didn't know the choice that faced him. He received world-class treatment and it might have been enough to give him an extra five or ten years of good quality life, taking care of his wife at home in Addis. He was able to come to Australia, to get to know his son-in-law Mel better, to see the life Sosi has made for herself, to see his son Yonatan again.

What would I have done in her place?

16

Lalibela

On the plane to Lalibela, Sosi, gazing out of the window, tells me how as a child she used to love the law, and would go to the courts in Addis to watch the female judges. I don't know what made her think of that. I don't know what relevance it has to anything in our story, except that it's something that she said, out of the blue, looking out of the window on that aeroplane, now that she, at last, after a year of caring for her father, fighting to have him treated in Australia and watching him die, didn't have to think of anything at all.

I can imagine Sosina as a judge, listening to all of the arguments, poker-faced, banging her gavel, not taking any crap, making stern pronouncements. But then I tend to imagine her standing up and doing a back bend on the bar, and the whole thing becoming a Dennis Potter screen musical like *The Singing Detective*, the court-room stenographers and illustrators waving side to side.

Sosina the chameleon.

Sosina the projection screen.

We are so glad to be in the air, floating above the Ethiopian plateau. The countryside is Australian-brown, hard-baked by the close sun, cut through with ravines and chasms creating arthritic fingers of land on which are dotted geometrically precise rectangular and circular village houses. Here and there a larger circle is a traditional church building.

Sosi, still gazing out the window, tells me about a documentary she saw that predicted the end of the world would come soon, on a certain date in 2012. All the planets were going to line up for the first time, and their combined gravity would make the world flip over. Or something like that. About the only country that would survive is Ethiopia (and maybe a couple of others she's forgotten). Not that she believes it, in particular: she's just saying.

It feels like we will never see a cloud.

Now Sosi tells me that back in the nineties an Ethiopian Airlines plane (like the one we're travelling on but bigger) crash-landed in the Comoro Islands near Madagascar. Three Ethiopian guys on the flight read in the free in-flight magazine in the seat back that Ethiopian airlines also flew to Australia. Considering this a more favourable destination, and proposing to seek political asylum, they decided to hijack the plane and force the pilot to change course. The pilot told them that there wasn't enough fuel to fly across the Indian Ocean to Australia, but they didn't believe him. Without telling them, he flew down the African coast, hoping he would be able to land somewhere safe. When the fuel ran out he was forced to land in the water near the Comoros. Many people on the flight died, either because they couldn't swim or because they inflated their life jackets inside the plane, floated to the roof and drowned.

All the stories heap up.

To imagine Lalibela Airport, picture a plain landing strip posted on the only flat spot in a vast and empty rocky landscape. Towering cliffs below high plateaux as backdrop. Box for terminal. Row of mini-vans in the carpark waiting to drive visitors the 25 kilometres to town.

We wheel our suitcases to the nearest mini-van. There, courtesy of Sosi, we soon meet Ephraim the driver and Mesfen the guide, both of whom have been hired by two English families whose mini-van we have accidentally gatecrashed. We sit up the front and chat to Mesfen while the English – parents and teenage children alike – look out at the very un-English landscape glumly.

I love to travel and now we're on this Lalibela jaunt I'm back in my element, as one of those tourists who feels superior to other tourists. When I travel I love to plan – because I get stressed about missing out on things or wasting time, about not having *the best possible* holiday (just like, for example, I get stressed out about my children not having the *best possible* childhood, which I think they partially appreciate and partially experience as me constantly harping on about things). Planning is so pleasurable because you can *control* things and minimise any risk of something bad happening like your father dying when you're six months old. My skillful planning, in this instance, is how we're confidently staying in the best-value hotel in town, as judged online by my statistically reliable fellow travellers (I had to text Linda in Australia to look that up for me, and she texted back the information, because it was too hard to find the Internet in Addis). But beyond the hotel booking, I can tell already that on this trip it's going to be best to go with Sosi's flow, and that's going to mean, unusually for me, a flow of people and relationships. I feel safe in her hands.

Mesfen is our first new friend. He's been working as a guide for twenty years. There's nothing he doesn't know about Lalibela, so Sosi says to him: 'Mesfen, actually, you know, there is an old lady here who I would love to find. My mother told me about this lady.

She used to run a bar and restaurant here, and she welcomed my father each time he visited Lalibela. The lady was so kind to him. They became great friends. She used to come to Addis Ababa too, and stay with my parents. And when my dad was able, eventually, to bring my mum here with him on one of his pilgrimages to Lalibela, the old lady gave my mum a present of some honeycomb. *You should look up this old lady if you can,* my mother said. She would be very old now if she were still alive.'

When Mesfen makes a not-sure face, Sosi calls up her mother and hands her mobile phone across to him. He listens and begins to nod.

'Yes,' he says now, 'I do know this lady who owned the guest-house. I can take you to her house. I've heard that she is not very well. She can't get out of bed. But we can go there when I have some time off on Sunday afternoon. I'm sure that we can find her.'

We pass some thatched stone huts – farmhouses – that look as African as all get up. Sometimes there is a cow or a goat standing in a stony paddock, a shepherd flicking a long stick at a flock of sheep or a bunch of kids playing with a makeshift ball. We wind by in our cramped capsule, gawking stupidly. We stop to take photos from a scenic lookout and a little girl in filthy clothes approaches us, clear eyed. It turns out that what she wants, most of all, is a pen. Like a modern day Greek god descending from Olympus I dispense a biro, but then the other kids want one and it all gets too confusing. I don't have any more spare pens. Should I give them money? Should I be helping one or helping all? Where would I stop? Now the anti-hero, I scuttle back to the safety of the minibus.

The stretched-out convoy of minibuses wends its way towards Lalibela along the otherwise empty one-lane road. If you can't afford a minibus ride – which you can't, most likely, unless you can also afford a plane ticket – you will be travelling on foot around here. As we get closer to town we notice more and more people walking alongside the road towards Lalibela. They walk one by one; in pairs, chatting; or in small groups. Some drive a single sheep or goat in front of them, others have donkeys bowed down with bags of grain across their backs. Some shoulder bags of grain themselves or carry a chicken or two in their arms. The men have wooden staffs, the women shawls and colourful parasols. It is a long walk and heavy carrying for some several kilometres into town but there is an air of anticipation in people's steps. It's Saturday: market day. The market will take place on the hillside beyond the churches, just as it has done every week for a thousand years. Two thousand, perhaps.

We slow down to pass a knot of people under glittering gold-tasseled umbrellas of red and green, blue and purple. Young men in pure-white cloaks lined with crimson and gold sing and dance to the beat of bongos. A wedding, Mesfen says. This weekend there's going to be a lot of weddings because soon it is the fasting season of Lent.

We drop off the English passengers and Mesfen at the Seven Olives Hotel, the oldest hotel in town, and Ephraim, our driver, takes Sosi and I on down the hill to our guesthouse. The main road through Lalibela has been upgraded recently, to torturous effect. In line with Lalibela's World Heritage status the government installed, instead of common or garden bitumen, authentic ye olde cobblestones, which in another thousand years or so will be charmingly worn and smooth but for this millennium are simply, overwhelmingly jarring. The van inches along, juddering, but it does mean that Sosi has more time to get to know Ephraim. Ephraim, who must be in his late teens, drives this minibus on the weekends for his elder brother. By the time we have arrived at our guesthouse, Sosi has a very good rapport indeed with Ephraim and is busy negotiating a flat rate of 1000 birr for him to be on-call to drive us around Lalibela for the next two days. The manager of the guesthouse wants to suggest a different minibus and driver but Sosi says, 'Well, we know Ephraim now. He's a nice guy and it would be good to help him; I think we should go with Ephraim.'

'Sure,' I say. I like Ephraim already.

Now we know Mesfen and we know Ephraim (Sosi has both of their numbers in her phone) and we have only just arrived in town.

Sosi and I eat lunch at a café across the road from the guesthouse called the Land of Promise, sitting outside in the front garden all alone. The whole place is deserted: the café, the street, adjacent shops. One old guy walks past with a moth-eaten donkey; after a while a couple of Japanese tourists come along the other way, each plopped in the saddle of a tourist horse, heading out of town to who knows where.

After lunch, Ephraim parks the minibus and leads us through the market on foot. We begin at the meat and livestock section where everything, actually, is livestock. Nothing is pre-butchered in this market (there's no refrigeration). If you want to eat lamb, buy a sheep. If you want to eat goat, buy a goat. We weave across a sloping paddock of bare dirt crowded with farmers, scrawny sheep and goats, all milling around together, catching up, as farmers, sheep and goats will do. Soon we come to an open area on the crest of the hill where women sit on the ground next to stretched-out cloths on which they have piled small mounds of *teff* or salt or the green vegetable they make into *tallah* (a homemade beer). There are no middlemen here: each farmer sells his or her own modest produce. Or hopes to sell: there appears to be a lot of very patient waiting and not much selling. Further up the hill, lines of makeshift stalls covered with plastic tarpaulin sell fabric, blankets and clothes, plastic and aluminium utensils. One stall sells old shoes, for which read *very old shoes*. Anything discarded that could still be of use to someone finds its way here. Even the most humble plastic container will be recognised for the work of genius it is. The whole marketplace, even with its plastic and its aluminium, feels positively biblical.

Each afternoon we eat lunch on the terrace of the Seven Olives. It's where Tewabé ate lunch, too, with Ayanalem, the time he brought her with him to Lalibela. The trees are thick with birds, the air reverberating with their cries. Our waitress is a beautiful young woman called Desta. Of course she becomes a kind of friend, too. Sosi discovers that she has come here from a town called Mekelle to work. She's trying to save some money but she only earns 300 birr (US$18) a month. Sosi slips her 100 birr in secret so that she doesn't have to surrender it to the tips jar, and tells her to be brave and follow through on what she wants in life. You go girl. Desta comes back later and asks Sosi for her email address so she can write to her.

I look across at Sosina relaxing in the cool air, chewing on her lunch.

'Do you think this is where the book should end?' I ask her.

We make two more friends in Lalibela (apart from the old lady).

Muluya, the first, is the young guide who shows us around the labyrinth of underground churches, once on the Saturday afternoon in tourist peak-hour and again on the Sunday morning before dawn when the rock chambers echo with chanting and pilgrims wrapped in white and shrouded in prayer stand motionless along the alleyways and walls around the churches.

The twelve ancient churches of Lalibela are strange indeed: dug out from the rock instead of built on top of it, they are freestanding, multi-storey structures styled and chiselled with geometrical precision. Each has its own distinct character. Some are gloomy and monumental while others are graced with delicate internal arches, high windows and painted ceilings.

Muluya explains to us that the entire complex was commissioned by the great King Lalibela in the twelfth century, with the aim of bringing Jerusalem to Ethiopia. Pilgrims were finding the long journey north to the original Jerusalem was hazardous, with wild animals, intemperate conditions and unfriendly heathens all standing in the way. Lalibela hit upon the idea of building his own Jerusalem at this remote site in the Ethiopian highlands. Between the two great clusters of churches, the king went so far as to commission the fashioning in the rock face of an artificial River Jordan snaking down the valley. It's all still there, a theme park for the divine.

The whole thing, says Muluya, took only twenty-seven years to complete: the River Jordan, all the churches and their interconnecting tunnels and walkways, including the tunnel called Hell, because it is pitch black, seems to go on almost forever and is hence like a precautionary foretaste of the real thing. The archaeologists wonder how, with the basic hand tools available in the twelfth century, this amazing speed of construction could have been possible, says Muluya, but the Church can explain this. Obviously the workers couldn't have done it by themselves. God saw they needed help. So, each night, after the workers knocked off in the evening, a crew of angels came in and took over the work. For twenty-seven years the workers worked the day shift and the angels worked the night shift. Well, how else do you explain such speed?

I am inclined as usual to be skeptical but Sosina, like Muluya, has an open mind. Sosina's able to juggle many worlds and stories.

The same slow, low chanting I could hear from the priests around Tewabé's coffin rings out from the underground churches of Lalibela long before dawn on Sunday morning. From our guesthouse apartment across the valley, we can't see the churches nestled in their holes so it seems as if the sound is emanating from somewhere deep within the earth. Sosi has given me the big front room with a view and taken for herself the more private room at the back. This is the first time we've ever shared an apartment, the two of us. Fleetingly and belatedly, it occurred to me that night, as Sosi padded past to the bathroom in her flannelette pyjamas and fluffy slippers, that our spouses, Mel and Linda, are very trusting. Luckily for all of us, our project has never been complicated by sexual tensions – that might make a good book, but it would be a very different book.

All through the labyrinth of churches that Sunday, the white-clad pilgrims are too engrossed in prayer and meditation to be bothered by the few tourists who drag ourselves out of bed to stumble past with our guides. 'See those bunk-sized holes cut into the rock walls beside the churches?' asks Muluya. 'That's where, in the old days, the dead would be buried, to lie close to the holy places.'

Inside one dimly lit church, a young bride and groom sit on the altar as if enthroned. Nothing much is happening. It looks like it is just another stopover for them in their day-long, week-long, month-long wedding rituals. All they can do is wait. It's hard to say if they look bored, preoccupied or nervous. Behind the curtain in another church lie the earthly remains of King Lalibela himself, or so we are informed. Needless to say, ordinary mortals aren't allowed backstage to peek at them, but we can request a spoonful or two of *holy soil* from the grave. A priest pours the holy soil into a folded piece of paper in Sosina's hand. If we can transport it safely back to Addis Ababa, the soil will be much appreciated by Ayanalem and, who knows, might help to cure her ailments or at least alleviate her suffering.

A boy called Bikis becomes our next friend. He has appointed himself to our service as shoe-carrier at the churches. Every time we stop to enter the solemn and mysterious confines of a church we have to leave our shoes outside. Bikis keeps them safe for us and accompanies us to the next. Muluya is an accredited guide who works for the Orthodox Church, which runs the whole show, but Bikis is just a high-school kid doing some opportunistic freelancing on the weekend and practising his English. He tells us he wants to be a doctor. Sosi, in what I now perceive to be her judge mode, offers no false hope. She tells Bikis: 'That will be very hard; you'll have to get good grades and go to Addis to study. Somehow find the money.' He nods. She gives him her mobile number and email address and often, once we are back in Addis, her phone will ring and she'll say: 'Hey Bikis...'

As the sun gets higher and we slip our shoes on again after visiting the last church, Muluya and Bikis lead us out through a crevice and down a narrow staircase etched into the rock to a flat area behind the church complex. Here we come across several groups of peasant farmers gathered together under the shade of straggly trees. Sosi wanders over to one group, who invite us to sit down with them and enjoy some home-made bread and *tallah*, the frothy brown foul-smelling fermented alcoholic drink, which a woman is ladling from a large plastic barrel. We accept the bread with pleasure but Sosi manages to explain that the *tallah* might upset my ginger Western stomach. Each group of farmers has its own spot, under these trees, where they meet up once a month while in town for the market. This is where, on a Sunday, they can relax, have a few beers, some bread, tell stories, gossip. Take turns to brew and bring the barrel of *tallah*. Pretty much what people everywhere do on a Sunday.

After his official duties with us are over Sosi invites Muluya to stop off with us for a coffee, and we get into another long political discussion about the Ethiopian government and the opposition, weighing up their pros and cons. When we say goodbye I give him my head torch, because I am learning generosity from Sosina: I can see it will be so useful for him (in the tunnel called Hell, for instance) and they are pretty much two-a-penny where I come from.

The old lady lives in the old World Heritage–stamped part of Lalibela, across the slopes beneath the Seven Olives, where crinkled paths wind past old stone houses. To arrive at the old lady's house we have to walk straight through another neighbourhood wedding: in a narrow laneway, trestle tables spread under old marquees, a knot of young folk dancing. As we draw closer Mesfen needs to ask directions; people nod and snake their hands ahead of us.

A middle-aged woman (the daughter?) meets us at the entrance to the old lady's house. The main room is perfectly clean but bare. One old dresser with a small glass cabinet on top holds a modest collection of crockery for display and special occasions: a few odd china plates, several water glasses, a little metal milk jug. The uneven walls are the brightest powder blue, a blue you could fall into. Through a faded red curtain we can see the old lady, curled away from us on a bed in a room the size of an alcove. Light streams in upon her, biblically again, from a window above the foot of the bed. Sosi is ushered in ahead of me. The old lady looks older than you can possibly imagine. She is tiny, wizened, curled up, blind. Any of her limbs you could snap like kindling.

Afterwards, Sosina recounts for me the conversation:

'Do you remember Tewabé?' she asks the old woman.

'Tewabé? Tewabé?' replies the old woman, with considerable effort.

'I am his daughter,' Sosi says.

'Tewabé?' repeats the woman, as if confused.

Then, miraculously, it's as if he pops up in some long-forgotten corner of her mind. She raises her head and reaches out her bony hand to clasp Sosina's.

'I know Tewabé,' she says. 'He's a good man.'

'I am his daughter,' repeats Sosina. 'The daughter of Tewabé and my mother, Ayanalem. She knows you, too. They say hello.'

(Once again, Sosi thinks it is kinder for the old lady to believe her father is alive.)

'Tewabé,' repeats the woman, caressing the name fondly now. 'He used to talk about a daughter; he called her Mimi,' she says.

'That's me!' says Sosi. 'That's me!'

And she gently grasps the old lady's tiny starling hand.

Tonight, after we return from Lalibela, Ayanalem is excited and wants to talk. She even says, *God willing*, she might come to visit Australia one day. She says Tewabé went to Lalibela seven times by road before he took her there on a plane to stay at the Seven Olives and sit on the same terrace we sat on, eating lunch. Tewabé knew so many people in Lalibela, Ayanalem says, they used to go visiting from house to house. Now the old lady is the only one left.

'Tewabé was a kind man,' says Ayanalem. 'He built this place for me — the hotel and restaurant — and he let me run it all.'

She looks at Sosi, dressed up in a short skirt, tights and boots, because we are going out to a restaurant.

'She has beautiful legs,' Ayanalem remarks to me. 'I used to have legs just like that. I used to wear a skirt shorter than that. A super-miniskirt. After we got married I wore skirts a little longer. My husband preferred that, so I said okay.'

Bikis calls Sosi again. Mesfen calls, too. Sosi chats with them, offering advice, encouraging them to take their chances.

Back in my now-familiar barely furnished bedroom at the Family Hotel, with the happy condom signs on the window, at the end of the corridor of love, I finally have time to think. What drew me to Sosina's story was the way that she continually confounds expectations. She refuses to live inside boxes made by others. She is a boundary crosser. Coming from this place without worldly power — Ethiopia — she somehow has it in her to generate her own. As for me, by contrast, a drama teacher at university once told me that I could make an excellent career as an actor playing victims. And yet, relatively speaking, I come out of power and privilege — a well-educated family in the bleached landscape of Perth's leafy western suburbs. So, what's that about? I suspect that I felt an affinity for victimhood because of the hidden story of my father: the primal story of the absence of his love and how I could neither change that, nor even express it. If I grew up inside a box it was one made from the silence in my family. It was only by writing the story of my father in my first book, in the form I wanted it to take, that I was able to finally extricate myself from that box. Now here in my 'not me' book I find myself in training with Sosina as she leads me out across the highwire.

On my last afternoon in Addis Ababa, we are standing at the gate of the Habesha restaurant in the Bole Road, waiting for Amaha to arrive. Sosi strikes up a conversation with the guard, who also does a basic form of valet parking. He's worked here seven years. The owner is a good boss, but he'd like to get a job as a driver so that he could be paid a little more and get home to see his family. This job is day and night, long hours, seven days a week. He asked Sosi's European NGO friend Jean Marc, who frequents this restaurant, for a job as his driver but Jean Marc has one already. Sosi says he should ask Jean Marc if he knows anyone else who needs one.

When we leave later after eating with Amaha we say goodbye warmly to the guard and wish him all the best. Amaha, who, Sosi suspects, has been drinking in the afternoon, sideswipes the gatehouse with the Corolla on the way out but accelerates away, unperturbed. Worse things have happened.

'Mel says I always think positively of people,' Sosi says. 'He can't believe it sometimes.'

Coda

There was one other thing that happened the last day I was in Addis. I bought a stove.

In Lalibela, you will recall, inspired by Sosi's generosity, I began to be uncharacteristically generous myself. As well as the head torch for Muluya, I gave Bikis the best-quality pen in my possession to aid him in his future studies. It's not much, I know, but it's the best thing I had. We also made sure to tip everyone handsomely.

By the time we arrived back at Ayanalem's house I was keen to go a step further. I wanted to leave behind something useful for the household, apart from money. Seeing the rows of hand-washed sheets and clothes draped all across the courtyard, I had the idea of buying a washing machine. I floated this tentatively with Sosina, but she said: 'We pay a local woman to come in and do the washing. It gives her a job. If you want to get something to help my mum, best thing would be a stove for Emuye. My mother would love that.'

A stove, I thought. *Okay, that sounds good.*

'Do you want to go look for one then?' said Sosina.

'Okay,' I said. 'Sure.'

Next thing Amaha dropped us at the best stove shop in town, in an up-market Addis mall, and I'm buying the best stove in the shop. $1000. I've got that in the bank. I can pay for it on a card. I feel a kind of giddy euphoria.

'My mum will love this,' says Sosina. 'Emuye the chef,' she's says, 'she's going to die!'

They deliver the stove before the close of business, before I have to get back into Amaha's car one last time to travel to the airport for my flight home to Australia.

It's not a fancy stove by Australian standards but in Emuye's kitchen it gleams like an alien spacecraft beside the gas bottles and single burners on the floor.

I can't quite believe that Sosi has picked up my warm and fuzzy thought bubble and helped me deliver it to her mother's kitchen before the close of business. But, as I've said, she's a can-do kind of woman.

Ayanalem cries. Emuye has a grin like Luna Park. She rushes off and insists on giving me, in return, her finest possession, a beautiful woven scarf.

I wasn't going to include the buying of the stove in the book, initially. Because now the story ends with me as the magnanimous hero bestowing my munificence on the Ethiopians in a burst of more-or-less random feel-good charity. As if I'm suddenly Bill Gates. As if I'm suggesting somehow that all the world's problems could be solved if comfortable First-world people like me saw the light, opened their wallets and waved money like a wand for poor Africans. (Although, frankly, good old random acts of kindness can be quite thrilling things to try when you have the opportunity.)

But I think that, no matter what else I do, I've now done one thing that was unequivocally worth doing. No matter what people might take it to mean symbolically, in that kitchen the stove is not a symbol. It's a stove, simple and pure. Sosi's mum could get by without a stove. Her household has managed without a stove for this long, just like most people in Ethiopia manage without a stove. They manage without a lot of things. The list of things they manage without becomes ridiculous when you start to think about it (for instance, say, electric milk-frothers). But to have several gas burners available simultaneously at your fingertips, at a comfortable height so you no longer have to crouch down on the floor, and with built-in trivets to hold your pots above the burners…To have an oven, for the first time, in which you can bake bread and cakes and roast meat…One of Sosi's young cousins, who Ayanalem and Tewabé have brought in from the country to go to school, has been doing cooking classes. Now she'll have somewhere to try out her recipes. Even now I'm back writing this in Australia, I think to myself, that gleaming little stove (which Sosina assures me Emuye will maintain for years to come in a perpetual state of gleam) is still there bubbling away in Ayanalem's kitchen half a world away, at the centre of that house which is also a hotel, restaurant and café.

On the plane home, an hour and a half from Melbourne. The middle of the night in some sped-up world high up in the sky. I have been thinking for a long time of how I will slip into bed beside Linda. I hand-washed my pyjamas in my room in Addis, hanging the top up one day on the pipe above the bathroom sink, the next day following with the pants. I have them folded in the outside pocket of my suitcase. I will have a shower downstairs, where nobody will wake and hear me. I will climb up the stairs and perhaps there will be moonlight. It might be hot, it being summer still in Melbourne. Linda will wake up when she's ready and I'll be home.

This thinking, in a funny way, is part of what Sosina's given me. I've learnt to have faith that I can take a leap into the unknown and still come home.

And what have I given her? Well, for a start, her spelling is appalling.

Sosina, meanwhile, never stops. Back home in Melbourne, she's jumping here and there. She's been cast in a feature film; her new baby, Kidus, has a small part, too. He has his own calls in the schedule, his own shots.

'What does he have to do?' I wonder. (He's only four months old.)

'Well, he has to lie down,' says Sosi. 'And he has costume fittings...'

I'm jiggling Kidus in his bouncer on her kitchen floor in St Albans. Raeey is having an afternoon nap. 'She was going a bit crazy,' says Sosina.

Sosi pads about the kitchen in her flannel pyjamas and fluffy slippers. This is her anti-Prada look. She's throwing together what could either be a late lunch or an early dinner (or, for that matter, an exceptionally late breakfast); she insists Linda and I stay and eat with her and Mel even though we are on our way out to see a play.

The acting job means she'll have enough money to return again to Addis; it's all happening with her new circus school. She wants to open it there next year. That's going to take some work.

She's tired but excited. Working twelve-hour days on the film plus a four-hour drive each way, expressing milk (not while driving)...

'Making a film is interesting,' she says. It's her first time doing 'straight' acting. She's always up for new experiences.

Meanwhile, I'm thinking, *We have to go now or we'll miss the show. She's never going to be able to cook this meal in time.*

But, somehow, of course, she does.

ACKNOWLEDGEMENTS

Invaluable noises of encouragement and words of wisdom came from many directions during the writing of this book. Along the way, I read parts aloud virtually whenever anyone would listen. I emailed chunks or sometimes the entire manuscript. Difficult questions also helped, of course: from acute first (and last) reader Linda Mickleborough, who helped bring Sosina and I together at the start; from my Varuna gang, Catherine Therese, Alice Nelson, Hayley Katzen, Amanda Webster, Kathryn Millard, Peter Bishop and Leah Kaminsky; from everyone at the Fairhaven writing residency and the Writers Victoria Nonfiction Workshop; from many others including Linda Funnell, Steven Amsterdam, Rose Michael, Vanessa Radnidge, Robin Hemley, Sydney Smith, Susan Hornbeck, Francesca Rendle-Short and Melissa Reeves.

A Varuna Second Book Fellowship gave the manuscript a precious kick-along early on, and introduced me to that extraordinary mesh of writers and to Sheila's cooking.

A grant from the Harold Mitchell Foundation enabled Sosina and I to travel to Ethiopia to stay with Sosina's family.

Julianne Schultz, editor of *Griffith REVIEW*, published a version of the chapter *The Cigarette Seller of Addis Ababa*.

My editor, Nicola Redhouse, once again shone a light on all the creaks and cracks, and helped me oil and patch them.

Terri-ann White, at UWA Publishing, said yes, and then proceeded with such passion, vision and good humour.

My wonderful colleagues at the nonfictionLab, the School of Media and Communication and elsewhere at RMIT University gave me time and support to write in between everything else, and held faith in the value of a book without footnotes.

Sosina's extended family and friends in Australia and Ethiopia fed, housed and entertained me with unfailing grace and kindness. My own family allowed me room to travel or to disappear to write, and greeted me with love when I returned.

Sosina herself, trusted.

SOURCES FOR QUOTATIONS

[p. 110] 'with the power of a father punishing a stubborn and disobedient son' and 'proceeded along the coast [of the lake] paddling to the sound of sonorous drums...':
Pakenham, Thomas 1992, *The Scramble for Africa*, Abacus: London, p. 27

[p. 123] 'weird cross between a kangaroo, a bicyclist, and a machine gun':
Rose, Phyllis 1991, *Jazz Cleopatra: Josephine Baker in her time*, Vintage: London, p. 19

[p. 123] 'We don't understand their language...':
Achard, Paul 1925, 'Trout en Noir ou la "Revue Negre"', Paris-Midi (27 September): Bibliotheque de l'Arsenal Pressbook (RO 15.702), Vols 1 and 2, quoted in Rose, Phyllis 1991, *Jazz Cleopatra: Josephine Baker in her time*, Vintage: London, p. 8

[p. 141–42] 'Among the rude tribes in this part of Africa...':
Mitchell, Augustus 1852, *Mitchell's Ancient Geography*, Thomas, Cowperthwait & Co: Philadelphia, pp. 58–59

[p. 143] The crafty Solomon...'worked his will on her' and 'The Imperial dignity shall remain perpetually attached...':
Ullendorff, Edward 1975, 'The Queen of Sheba', in *The Dictionary of Ethiopian Biography*, Institute of Ethiopian Studies: Addis Ababa, p. 153

Printed in Australia
AUOC02n1807310315
266714AU00004B/4/P

9 781742 586786